MW01141607

# Realm of Memory

a memoir

Copyright © 2019 Alice Woodrome

All Rights Reserved

# Preface

Although a true story, some creative license has been taken in writing this memoir. At times memories that were little more than snapshots were expanded into scenes. Names that could not be recalled are fictitious, and the timeline is somewhat rearranged. Through the pages, however, the emotional truths have been faithfully recorded.

## Hometown
## April, 2019, Friday, Late Afternoon

"This is probably the last time we'll come back to Quincy." I cross my arms and draw them close to my body as my younger sister slows the car to cross the bridge into Illinois. I sigh. "There won't be any more funerals to attend, and who knows how many more years we have left."

Chris keeps her eyes focused on the road. "True enough, sis. When we saw David last spring, I sure didn't expect it would be the final time."

I roll down the passenger window to smell the fresh spring air and gaze down into the muddy depths as we drive across the wide Mississippi River. A pleasure boat speeds by a string of barges in the channel as the air horn of a tugboat blares. We spent so many hours on those waters when we

were children; the river means *home* to me—
maybe as much as the house where we grew up.

From the bridge we take Main Street and head east
into Quincy. I glance at Chris. "Seems strange,
doesn't it? Just the two of us now."

Peering over her sunglasses, she nods in
melancholy agreement.

Chris and I, in our seventies, are all who remain of
our family of five. Our older brother recently
joined Mama and Daddy in the realm of memory.

David and I haven't been close since we were
teenagers—separated by six hundred miles,
different interests, and sensibilities. He and his
wife, Rose, lived in Springfield, not far from her
family, who still live in Quincy. Dave had found a
good match in Rose after a disastrous first
marriage, and I'd been happy for them.

When Rose called me months before in January,
an instant chill had coursed through me. My
brother had always been the one who phoned me
on the rare occasions I heard from them.

"I hope I'm not calling too early, Alice, but Dave
didn't wake up this morning," Rose told me,
remarkably composed. "I assumed he was sleeping
in—he's been pretty tired lately, but not really ill."
David was already cold when Rose finally went in

to rouse him. She'd called me while the police were still there.

His body was cremated, but she postponed the memorial in our hometown until April because of icy weather. The shock of his sudden death has passed, but I haven't yet come to terms with the reality that a few ashes, some photos, and memories are all that's left of my big brother.

As we drive past Washington Park and the old stone library, it troubles me that I am not feeling more than I am. David was only two years older, and we grew up together. I should be heartsick, mourning his passing with tears, but my emotions are so tangled I can't tease out the grief.

Perhaps coming home will help—a time to remember and say goodbye, not just to Dave, but to Quincy.

A breeze sweeps in my open window, and I catch the scent of ornamental pear trees blooming outside a business.

We drive through the downtown historic district, past brick and stone buildings, some erected before the Civil War. They now house clothing stores, a bank, cafes, offices, and antique and specialty shops. As we travel farther east, commercial structures give way to stately mansions in ornate styles built in the 1800s.

We pass the junior high school we attended, a Gothic masterpiece with pillars and arches, constructed in the 1930s. Chris points to a gargoyle at the corner of the majestic edifice. "It's amazing how we took all these magnificent old buildings for granted when we were growing up."

I crane my neck to see, marveling at the spectacular flourishes. "It was all just part of the backdrop of our childhood."

Chris takes off her sunglasses as we traverse a street shaded by the arching limbs of huge trees on either side.

"Let's swing around town after we put our stuff in the room," I say as we head toward the Holiday Inn. "It'll be nice to see everything again, just in case we never make it back."

She turns to me and smiles. "Yeah, six hundred miles would be a long trip if it was only to drive down memory lane."

The memorial open house is scheduled for Saturday afternoon, giving us this evening and tomorrow morning to visit the places that hold our childhood memories.

We check into the hotel on a road that looks completely different than it did fifty years ago. It seems odd to be a stranger in the town where we grew up. Our relatives have either died or moved away except for one cousin, who is in ill health. Even my friends from high school are gone.

On the way up in the elevator from the lobby, I say, "Did you notice how the desk clerk directed his questions to you?" I laugh. "I think I've been mistaken for your little, white-haired mother again."

Chris smirks. "Well, if you'd gain about fifty pounds to smooth out your wrinkles…"

It's happened often enough that we get a kick out of the reaction when we correct someone who makes the assumption aloud. My black hair went silver in my fifties like our aunt Emma's, but Chris —only fifteen months younger—takes after our dad, with hair almost as dark as when she was a kid.

We grab a quick bite to eat in the hotel restaurant, then head to Chris's Cadillac to swing by our old haunts.

I settle into the passenger seat. "Where shall we go first?"

"Let's start at the beginning—the house where we lived before I went to school?"

"That's not the first place *I* remember," I say. "But I just have one hazy memory from there. Several people were celebrating outside in the street—cheering and whooping it up. It must have been when World War II ended."

"Wow, Alice. That would be 1945. I would have been about a year old." Chris starts the engine. "Where was the place?"

"I don't have a clue." I laugh. "I was only two, you know. I think we moved not long after."

"Okay, so I guess we start at the house before Adams Street." She grabs her sunglasses from the cup holder. "Do you remember where that one is?"

"Not exactly. We were still pretty young when we moved from there. You would have been four or five. But Daddy drove us back there once a few years later. I think I can get to the neighborhood." I gesture toward the west. "That way."

Chris takes a right out of the Holiday Inn parking lot onto Broadway. "I'd never be able to find it," she says.

"Turn at the next light." I point. "The area was nothing but a slum when we lived there. Do you remember the garbage dump across the alley?"

"No—the surroundings are a blank." Chris frowns. "All I can picture is the yellow-linoleum floor in the kitchen. Oh, and the steps down to the little porch where Mama fell once, and the backyard."

We drive through the area where our family rented a place before I started first grade. "I doubt I'll recognize the old house even if it looks the same," I say.

Poverty and neglect still mark the neighborhood—peeling paint, graffiti, and overgrown shrubs. Some places are abandoned and boarded up. In front of a shack with a door hanging from one hinge, a small boy shoves a stick into the wet dirt. A tricycle with two wheels leans against a rusty bed frame in the brown weeds.

Hazy memories surface, but the nostalgia I expect to feel is overshadowed with the realization that some people never escape these pitiful conditions. Our own grandparents hadn't. I push the thought down.

"I don't see any outhouses. At least that's an improvement." I shake my head. "It's hard to fathom that we once lived like this."

"I'm glad we got out while we were still little."

We drive through the neighborhood for a few minutes, past houses, duplexes and a corner convenience store. While it all appears oddly familiar, nothing specific stands out. "I don't see anything that looks quite right," I say.

Chris sighs. "I hoped maybe you'd know our old

house when you saw it. I remember so little about living there."

A shiver runs up my arms at the reality of the deprivation. "Let's get out of here. It's giving me the creeps."

We end up parking in a cemetery overlooking the Mississippi and stroll among the graves of the long dead. My sister has always adored old graveyards, and when we travel together, we usually find one. I think it's the history they represent; she likes antique shops for the same reason. Chris traces a hand over the pitted top of a granite gravestone, her eyes pensive.

The 45-acre Woodland Cemetery in Quincy, bounded by an ancient wrought-iron fence, is as scenic as any we've visited. Mature oak trees and maples grace the rolling green hills dotted with antiquated tombstones. Given the solemn nature of this weekend, it seems odd that I feel more peace here than sadness.

Chris points at a grave. "This woman died the year I was born." She snaps a picture of the mossy stone dated *1877-1944*.

I pause at a bluff with a panoramic view of the mile-wide river and take a picture with my phone. "I should have gotten at least one shot of the old neighborhood. It's too bad I couldn't find the house."

"I bet it was torn down long ago."

"It was crumbling when we lived in it." I shrug. "There aren't many good memories from there, anyway."

We stroll along the walkway through a section with small gravestones sitting at odd angles with dates in the 1800s. We pass under an ancient oak tree with budding leaves the size of squirrels' ears.

Chris turns to me, raising her brows. "I know we didn't have much, but I was happy. Weren't you?"

"I suppose—mostly, anyway."

"Well, I was."

I frown. "But you said you hardly remember the place."

"I remember the jungle gym Daddy built in the backyard. I loved that."

"You were a regular monkey." I laugh.

Chris grins. "It was pretty neat."

"Daddy could always build about anything he put his mind to."

She glances at me with a wistful smile. "Or fix

anything."

I nod and take a deep breath. "I think maybe he could have."

Chris wanders off the walkway and steps around a small gravestone. "I sometimes wonder what Daddy would have become if he hadn't quit school after eighth grade to help Grandpa."

"Who knows?" I stop to snap a picture of the sun peeking through the branches of a huge oak tree. "I suspect he learned a lot more on the farm than he would have in a classroom—and more when he built things in the Civilian Conservation Corps— practical things, anyway."

"Yeah, I'm sure that's true."

"But Daddy was a wiz even before the CCC. Remember him talking about Grandma's washing machine when he was a kid?"

She cocks her head. "I don't think so."

"When it broke, Daddy said he begged Grandma to let him have the motor to play with. He had some project he wanted it for—a go-kart, I think—if he could fix it."

"Did he get it running?"

"Yeah, but Grandma reneged, and told him to put

it back on the washer."

"Gee, that wasn't fair."

I snicker. "Maybe not, and he probably wasn't very happy about it, but his mother needed a washing machine more than he needed a go-kart, and they couldn't afford to buy a new one."

As we walk, I pluck a leaf off a low-hanging branch. "Daddy's folks eventually lost the farm, anyway, even with the money from the CCC. Times were bad all over. I wish I could remember all the stories he and Mama told about those days during the Depression, but I only recall bits and pieces."

"Me too. Seems a shame. I don't recall Mama talking much about her childhood, but I'll never forget that place where her parents lived." Chris purses her lips and shakes her head. "Sad. That house was barely standing and looked like it should have been condemned."

"I think Mama just wanted to forget those years, and that's why she resisted talking about them. Twelve siblings born and only five survived. That tells you something." I meet my sister's eyes. "You know those seven didn't all die of disease." The skin on my arms prickle. "Grandpa Harry was responsible for at least one death, maybe another."

"Honestly?" Chris's mouth falls open and her hand flies to her chest. "I knew he was a mean drunk, but… Oh, my gosh! What happened?"

"I never learned the details, but it was his drinking —and his temper. The story I heard was that he pushed Grandma down the stairs when she was pregnant, and the baby was born dead—a little boy. He buried him in their yard and didn't report it to anyone. Mom was six. He'd be arrested today." I shake my head. "Their first child, Charlie, died when he was about a year old. He got pneumonia after Grandpa Harry took him out in the cold without a coat or hat."

"I had no idea." Chris groans. "I can't imagine how Grandma felt."

"Whether or not it was Grandpa's fault, I don't know," I add, "but that was the story. The rest of them succumbed to different diseases—smallpox, whooping cough, measles. I can't recall the list. The seven who died were all boys but one, and the girl died of what they called *crib death* then."

"Did Grandpa have a job? I don't remember anyone ever saying."

"Part of the time he did. My guess is he didn't keep one very long when Mom was growing up. I don't know how they made ends meet with five kids to feed. I think Grandpa Harry's mother lived with them for a few years before her death and collected a widow's pension from the Civil War."

We walk for a while in silence through the peaceful graveyard. It strikes me that although my sister and I live close to each other and talk nearly every day, we focus on the present at home, and rarely discuss the distant past. It's almost like our lives in Oklahoma are unrelated to the early experiences that are center-stage here in Quincy.

"I didn't realize *how* poor we were at the time," Chris says, "but Mama and Daddy gave us some great memories, didn't they?"

"Yeah, I think they tried to be good parents despite not having much in the way of role models—or material things to offer. Mama wanted us kids to have a better childhood than her own. I'm sure that's why she couldn't wait to get out of that neighborhood."

"I wish I could remember more about that house," Chris says, "I just have snapshot memories before we moved to Adams Street."

I remember much more.

# Rats
## Mid-1940s

Early morning light filtered through the kitchen
curtains onto the yellow, plastic tabletop. I sat with
my brother and sister eating breakfast. David had
already dressed. He was in first grade, but Chris
and I weren't old enough for school yet, and we
were still in our jammies. Daddy was in his
bedroom getting ready to go to the factory.

Mama shrieked. "Rats!"

I dropped my spoon and spun around. My mama
was looking at something along the baseboard.

"Those are too big for mouse droppings. I *thought*
I heard noises in here last night." She stood, put a
fist on her hip, and turned toward the hall. "Bob!
Bob!"

Daddy hurried from the bedroom, frowning, his
tan work shirt half-buttoned. "What is it, Lola?"

"Rats have been in my kitchen." Mama looked like
she was about to cry. "See that?" She pointed to
the evidence on the faded yellow linoleum. "I

won't live with those nasty things."

Mama said rats were filthy and made people sick, so I didn't want them in our house either. I had seen a rat for the first time when our neighbor's dog caught one a few weeks before. Skipper wasn't a big dog, but he could sure run. He was always catching something—usually a mouse—but I heard he got baby rabbits too and even chased down a squirrel once. I liked dogs, but I didn't like him killing bunnies or squirrels. Skipper's owner, Mr. Kemper, told me running after critters was in his nature because he was a fox terrier. He carried the rat around in his mouth like it was some treasure. It was big and ugly with a pointy nose and naked tail. It made me shudder to think about those nasty critters in our kitchen at night.

"I'll get some traps. You won't have to worry about them much longer," Daddy told Mama while she swept up the droppings. "I got a good deal on the lumber, so I've already ordered it out. I'll be framing our new house before you know it." He sat at the table, and Mama placed a bowl of oatmeal in front of him.

"With no help and working full time? It'll still be months before it's built." She sat down and looked him in the eyes. "I'm getting so tired of living like this, Bob."

He sighed and brought a hand to his forehead. "I

realize it don't look like it, but I've already done a lot of the hard work. We have a good solid foundation now. I just got a little more to do—then it will go fast."

Mama wrung her hands. "It's just that it's already taken so long. I know it'll be a good house when you finish, but it's been almost a year since we bought the lot, and the kids are getting older. Alice starts school next year. This is not a respectable neighborhood to grow up in."

Mama always talked about being *respectable*. We wore hand-me-down clothes, but she kept them mended and washed. She was a good cook too. I especially liked it when she made dumplings for dinner or ham hocks and potatoes. We all sat down together, and she reminded us of our manners. "Elbows off the table," she said. "Napkin on your lap." And if we said something wrong like *ain't,* she corrected us every time. But Mama wanted to move into what she called a *decent* neighborhood and reminded Daddy of that all the time. I wasn't sure how a *decent* neighborhood was different from where we lived, but I wanted Mama to be happy.

"I'll pick up the rat traps today. We'll catch'em." Daddy hugged Mama. "Try not to worry about it, honey," he said and left for the factory. She winced as the screen door slammed behind him.

I never saw a rat trap before, but they looked like big mouse traps. I heard a racket in the kitchen the first night Daddy set them. The next morning, David told me a rat didn't get killed outright, and was dragging the trap around. He saw it all. I didn't ask what happened next and had to put my hands over my ears when he described what Daddy did with the rat. I didn't like rats, but I still felt sorry for it.

Daddy caught two rats that week and plugged up a hole under the sink and several other places he thought they might sneak in.

"I still hear them scratching at night," Mama told Daddy at breakfast one morning the following week. "It sounds like they're up in the attic."

"At least they're not in the house," Daddy said. "Right now that's the best I can do. We can't kill every rat in the neighborhood."

"Well, I guess that's true," Mama said, and with a bitter edge, she added, "Not with a dump across the alley."

"We can get a dog like Skipper," I said, even though I knew Mama wouldn't go for it.

I grinned at Chris. Her big brown eyes sparkled.

Mama shook her head. "Dogs are too much trouble." She held up a finger. "But cats—they're independent. Emma is looking for homes for some of hers." My aunt had a whole family of cats, the kittens nearly grown.

I clapped my hands. "Can we have one, Daddy, can we?" I couldn't wait. A cat was soft and cuddly and if you dragged a string, it would chase it.

"Couldn't hurt to have a cat around, I guess."

All three of us kids cheered.

My uncle brought over the cat from Aunt Emma that week, and we named her Snowflake. She was pure white with a pink nose and pretty green eyes. It took a few days before Snowflake would play with me. But once we got acquainted, she purred when I petted her. I could tell she liked me because she rubbed against me a lot.

I don't know if Snowflake caught any rats or not. She wasn't much bigger than one herself. We'd barely had her two weeks, and then one day, she disappeared.

I called and called up and down the street, crying when I couldn't find her.

"You've looked long enough," Mama said. "I don't want you out wandering around in this neighborhood."

"But Mama, Snowflake hasn't been home for two

days. Maybe she's lost and doesn't know her way back. I gotta find out where she is!"

I heard her talking to Daddy that evening about Snowflake and how upset I was. "Sometimes it's best not to know things," she said to him. "Ignorance is bliss."

## April, 2019, Friday Evening

My sister and I walk past a small mausoleum in the old cemetery. The blossoms on a dogwood tree flutter as a gust of wind brushes its graceful branches.

"Did they ever find out what happened to Snowflake?" Chris asks. "I don't even remember the cat."

"No one told me if they did," I say. "I didn't know then what Mama meant by 'ignorance is bliss,' either."

"Makes me wonder," Chris says, "if Mama knew what became of Snowflake and just didn't want to say."

A thought strikes me I had never considered. I look at Chris. "You know, Snowflake wasn't the only cat that disappeared in that old neighborhood—and I doubt that Skipper was the only culprit."

Chris cocks her head. "What do you mean?"

"Tom. Remember him? He was that neighbor kid a

few years older than us. They lived on the other side of the Kempers. Boy, was he bad news. I only have one clear memory of Tom, but it's enough."

"I do remember Tom. I didn't like him," she says.

I shook my head. "You don't know the half of it."

## Innocents
## Late-1940s

Sparrows twittered in the branches above me on that spring day. Mama said I was old enough at five to play in the backyard while she was in the kitchen. I sat in the sandbox under the oak tree pretending to make a cake.

"Eleven, twelve, thirteen," I counted as I scooped sand with a blue plastic shovel into a red bowl cradled between my open legs. I knew my numbers all the way to fifty.

"Hey kid." Tom's voice startled me. Fences didn't separate the yards in our neighborhood, and Tom, about twelve, had retrieved many balls from our backyard. I looked up.

He sauntered toward me in frayed and faded overalls with a torn pocket.

The only thing I knew about Tom was what Daddy had grumbled to Mama once. Twisting his lip, he'd said, "That boy ain't right."

I didn't know what he meant, but it didn't matter.

Tom never played with kids my age. That's why it seemed strange when he walked right up to me.

"Wanna see something keen?" Tom towered over me where I sat in the sand.

I shaded my eyes with my hand and looked up. "What?"

"Baby mice." He ran his fingers through his unruly brown hair. "A whole nest of them." Pointing to the back of their yard, he added, "They're over in our shed."

I'd never seen baby mice. I liked babies, so I stood up and dusted the sand off my pants.

"Is their mama there, too?" I followed Tom over the railroad ties between our yards. I had to hurry to keep up with him.

"Just the babies." He led me down the walk to his shed. "She probably got scared off."

He opened the door, and I stepped into the shed behind him. Sunshine filtered through cracks in the timbers, throwing stripes of light across Tom's back. It took a moment for my eyes to adjust to the darkness. Saws, rakes, and garden tools hung on the walls, and in the back sat the lawn mower I'd seen Tom's father push around his yard. Spider webs spanned the corners, and the air smelled of rotting grass and gasoline.

"They're over here," Tom said in a breathless voice. He bent over a tattered cardboard box on its side with a Caltex motor oil label. A tangle of shredded paper filled the box.

My stomach fluttered in anticipation. "Where's the babies?" It just looked like trash.

"They're in there." He pulled apart some jumbled paper strips to show me.

I caught my breath. Several baby mice nestled together in a rosy ball inside the maze of shredded paper, moving enough that I knew they were real and alive. Their eyes were closed, and they had no fur, just naked, little bodies smaller than peanuts.

"They're so cute." I crouched, in awe of the tiny creatures snuggled together, all soft and pink and perfect.

"Now comes the fun," Tom said. "Watch."

I moved closer and watched the babies carefully.

Behind me, I heard a scratch and smelled a lit match.

Tom laughed and threw it into the nest.

I caught my breath, frozen in horror as the babies squeaked and scratched trying to escape the flames.

My heart raced. I started to shake and could hardly breathe. I turned to look at Tom's face twisted in a grin, and I began to cry.

"You're... terrible," I shouted.

He just kept grinning. I ran from the shed as fast as I could.

# April, 2019, Friday Evening

Chris's eyes widen, her hand covering her mouth. "Oh, no!"

I shake my head slowly as we stop to rest on a cemetery bench. "The image of those innocent little creatures squirming in pain is seared into my memory."

"How could anyone *ever* forget such a thing?" She crosses her arms. "That's just evil! Now *I* won't be able to forget it either." She meets my eyes. "Did you tell Mama or Daddy?"

I shake my head. "I was too upset, and I thought I might get in trouble." I shudder. "I can still see Tom's face when he saw my reaction. He was delighted."

"That's awful—horrible! But I'm not surprised. He enjoyed hurting people, too. He tripped me on purpose once when I was learning to roller skate. I fell hard on the sidewalk, cutting my knee. He just laughed at me as I sat there crying with my leg bleeding."

A breeze sweeps through the cemetery, rattling the branches above us and chilling my arms.

"I wonder whatever happened to Tom," I say. "I think we moved the next year. That was right before I started first grade. I'd like to think he grew out of that kind of meanness."

"I sort of doubt it," Chris says. "I'm glad we got out of that neighborhood when we did." She turns to me with an elbow cupped in one hand and a fist resting against her chin. "Hey, why didn't Daddy ever finish building our house? I just remember moving to the house on Adams Street. I was pretty little."

"Bad luck, naivety, impatience… take your pick." I glance at her. "I don't know all the details. Mama and Daddy didn't tell us everything."

## Moving
## Late-1940s


One Saturday evening as cornbread baked in the oven and bean soup simmered on the stove, I helped Mama set the table. I felt clever for knowing how to put the forks and spoons in their proper places.

The door swung open, and Daddy took a weary step inside. He kissed Mama and slumped into a chair at the table. "They delivered the lumber while I was at the lot today," he said. "It's warped —way too warped."

Mama's eyes went round. "What do you mean?" She sat down, her hand on her mouth. "Too warped to use?"

"More than half of it ain't good for nothing but firewood, and the rest is almost as bad." He pressed his lips together tight, his nostrils flaring.

Mama's hand went to her chest. "They need to give your money back."

Daddy shook his head. "The sale was final 'cause I

got a good price. I should've looked it over careful instead of trusting the guy who sold it to me." He huffed a breath.

Mama looked close to tears. "But Bob, it took us so long to save up for that lumber." She grasped his arm, her face turning red. "They have to give you your money back. They just have to. Talk to the man!"

"I did, dammit," Daddy snapped and his fist hit the table. "I went over there straight away." He shook his head. "There's no two ways about it. We're stuck with lumber we can't use."

The shout brought David into the kitchen. He looked at our parents, and then at me with a question in his eyes. I drew my shoulders up and shook my head.

Tears came to Mama's eyes, and she jerked to her feet and went to stir the soup. "We'll never get out of this dump. It'll always be something."

I wanted to hug my mother because she was so sad. But she was angry too, so I didn't want to be too close. I straightened a spoon on the table and walked to the other room with my brother.

"Daddy doesn't like the lumber for the new house," I whispered to Dave. "He said a bad word."

My parents barely spoke while we ate our bean soup, but I could tell Mama was still mad by the way she breathed heavy and wouldn't look at Daddy. He slouched over his bowl, and said only a word or two during supper. David and I kept quiet too, but Chris didn't seem to notice Mama's mood.

"I saw Mr. Kemper's dog with another rat today, Daddy," Chris blurted out.

Mama slammed her napkin down hard, got up, and left the room.

"Is Mama mad at me?" Chris asked, looking at Daddy.

"She's upset about something else, honey," he said. "Finish up your supper, and you and Alice can help me do the dishes for Mama."

That was the only time I ever remember Daddy washing dishes.

The next day Mama told me Daddy wouldn't build a house for us after all. We were going to find one already built.

A few evenings later, Daddy took us to look at a place in the old German neighborhood in the south part of town. Mama was mostly German, but I don't know if that played into the decision. We drove to a street lined with tall leafy trees and a tavern on the corner. The yards had neatly trimmed grass, and some had flower beds too. The houses didn't have junk in the front like at home. Some people were sitting out in lawn chairs visiting with neighbors. We parked outside a small wooden house and got out of the car.

Mama looked up and down the block. "Nothing fancy about it, but it's a respectable neighborhood."

We followed Daddy up the walk and around the house to look at the backyard. It was long and narrow with a cracked cement path that led down to a shed. Garages and other outbuildings lined the alley at the back of the yards. The houses had clotheslines behind them and a few had vegetable gardens.

"Not bad, don't you think?" Daddy said. "I like the yard, and that shed will come in handy."

Mama pointed to the outhouse. "You know I don't want an outhouse," she said.

"That's not a big problem," Daddy said as he opened the unlocked backdoor. "It's an old house, but we can afford it.

Mama frowned as we toured the empty rooms. She looked out the kitchen window toward the alley. "I like to look out on the street when I'm cooking, not the backyard."

"But that's a great backyard. And everything else is pretty much just what we need." Daddy waved his hand around the room. "For a small house, it's got a nice big kitchen, even a pantry. You'll like that." He raised his brows and leaned toward Mama.

"What about the outhouse?" Mama said. "You know I want an indoor bathroom like proper folks. I don't see any other outhouses on this whole block."

His confidence didn't waver. "I could put a toilet room inside."

I looked at Chris and grinned. A bathroom inside the house would be great. I hated the outhouse, worried that spiders would bite my bottom when I sat down. In the winter, it was freezing.

"But the kitchen." Mama folded her arms across her chest. "I'd still have a kitchen at the back of the house."

He put his arm around her shoulder. "I'll change the rooms any way you want them, Lola." His face brightened. "I could build you nice cabinets for your dishes, too—any color you want—and lay new linoleum on the floor." I could tell he was trying hard to make Mama feel better.

With Daddy's promise to install a toilet inside and

switch the rooms around to suit her, Mama agreed.

They arranged to buy the house, and Daddy set to work on his new project soon afterward. It took him only a few weeks to swap the rooms and build Mama's kitchen cabinets.

We moved in before the indoor toilet replaced the outhouse, but Daddy accomplished that a week or so later, and Mama was happy. We even heard her singing while she cooked in her new kitchen.

# April, 2019, Friday Evening

Across the river, the sun is sinking lower in the sky and the shadows cast by the gravestones lengthen. My sister and I pick up our stroll through the cemetery.

"We probably ought to get back to the hotel before long," I say. "It's going to be dark soon, and I'm not crazy about being in a graveyard at night."

"I wish we had time to see the little house on Adams now," Chris says, as we turn to head toward her car, "but it's been a long day."

"I wonder if the people who live there still have the rooms the way Daddy rearranged them."

"With that odd layout, I somehow doubt it." Chris smiles. "I never realized how strange it was until years later. I mean who has their front door open into the master bedroom or a sink in the corner of the kid's room?"

I shake my head slowly. "We must have been so young we just accepted things. It never occurred to me at the time how weird it was that Daddy shaved every morning in our bedroom or that the rest of the family washed up there."

"We did all need a place to wash. I'm sure that's why he left the old kitchen sink in."

"And poor David," I say. "I don't know how they squeezed his bed into the old pantry; both ends touched the walls. And how many other kids had a door in the floor of their bedroom that led to a fruit cellar or had to go through their sisters' room to get to the rest of the house?"

"Or a toilet room in the kitchen's corner." Chris's grin turns into a chuckle. "We heard every fart and flush when someone had to excuse themselves to go to the bathroom during mealtime."

I laugh. "It may have been odd, but I was happy there. I never thought to compare our house to anyone else's until I was grown. I guess Mama was right—sometimes ignorance really is bliss."

For a few minutes we stroll in silence.

"I wonder how Daddy felt about having to abandon building a house for us." Chris pushes the fob button to unlock her car. "He never wanted to be in debt, and I bet he hated making mortgage payments."

"He never seemed bitter." I open the passenger side and get in. "It would have taken a long time to save up for more lumber. Mama would have been hard to live with if they hadn't been able to sell the lot and put a down payment on a place in a better neighborhood. Daddy was a practical man. He knew when to capitulate."

The sun is nearly to the horizon on the other side of the Mississippi. "We can drive down Adams tomorrow," Chris says. "We'll have all morning to see what we want to see, and I don't want to rush it if it will be our last time in Quincy."

"The morning light will be nice, too," I say. "We can get some great photos."

"We'll get an early start. There's a lot to see. And I'll want to spend some time in the park; maybe walk along the creek again." Chris buckles her seat belt and we take the winding drive out of the cemetery. "Amazing now when you think about it —how Mama let us spend all afternoon at the park alone. It's a different world now."

"I'm glad we didn't have to wait for Mama to go with us." I click my own seat belt into place as we turn out onto the street and head north toward the hotel. "I wonder if there are really more dangers now, or if we just know more about them."

She sighs. "I'm not sure, but I'd hate to be raising kids now."

"Especially with the Internet," I say, as a woman in the car passing us talks on her phone. "Seems the entire world lost its innocence when the Internet came along."

Chris shakes her head. "You know, the little kids in the neighborhood look at me like I'm a threat when I walk by and say hello. They are so suspicious, they can't even say hi to an old lady." She looks at me. "We're starting to sound like old fogies."

I laugh. "We are old fogies."

# April, 2019, Saturday Dawn

The sun is barely up the next morning as we head to the south part of Quincy. Gold and scarlet streak the eastern sky, bathing everything in a warm hue. Long shadows stretch from trees and houses. I sip a cup of coffee in the passenger seat, already feeling sentimental as we drive through streets that have changed little in the last few decades.

"To Adams Street first," Chris says, passing the familiar houses along the mile-long stretch of Twelfth Street, the route we walked to junior high so long ago. She makes a right turn at the corner where later we waited for the school bus to attend senior high.

Chris drives down the humble street and pulls to a stop across from the little house that was our home until we left for college. The off-white frame structure has been painted fairly recently, but the shrubs are dead, at least the ones visible from the street. A satellite dish sits mounted on one corner of the gray metal roof.

"This is really where most of my memories began." Chris's voice is wistful.

I nod. "Me too, really." I take a picture of our old house. A curtain in the front window gaps open for a moment and then falls back.

"They're up early too," Chris says. "I bet the people who live there are wondering what we're doing out here. I'm tempted to knock on the door and tell them we grew up here and ask if we can look inside."

"That would take a lot of nerve." I stare at the house that holds so many memories. "I'm not sure I want to see inside, anyway. I'd rather remember it the way it was."

"Let's drive down the alley and see the backyard." Chris pushes the ignition button and pulls away from the curb.

She parks in the alley next to the old shed. I take a few photos of the back of the house and the yard.

"Look, they still hang clothes out to dry." I motion toward a string of shirts and jeans swaying in the breeze from a clothesline. "That sure brings back memories. Every Monday like clockwork."

"I bet the lady who lives there doesn't wash them in a wringer washer like Mama did," Chris says, "or make their clothes on a push-pedal sewing machine. She probably doesn't cook all their food from scratch either."

I nod. "And I doubt if they grow the vegetables they eat."

Our parents worked hard. Daddy was a maintenance man at a factory, but was always busy at home too. I looked at the side of the yard where he grew a vegetable garden, recalling the rows of lettuce, tomatoes, and green beans. I'd especially liked the big line of corn for roastin' ears and the rows of potato hills.

"Do you remember us kids helping Daddy when he dug the potatoes out of his garden?" I ask.

"Sure. We made a game out of it. It was great fun, but I think David usually won. He had the longest arms and biggest hands."

I smile, picturing in my mind Daddy turning over a pitchfork of soil and us kids scrambling to see who could find the most spuds before he went to the next hill.

"And that squash he grew." Chris chuckles. "It sprawled all over the garden. He harvested way more zucchini and yellow squash than we could eat. I don't think we even liked it."

I laugh. "I'm sure that's why zucchini bread was invented. I think he gave most of the squash to neighbors, though. They probably didn't like it either, but it always came with home-grown tomatoes, so…"

"Ah, yes, the tomatoes," Chris says. "Mama put a ton of them up in jars every summer."

"And a mountain of green beans, too. The kitchen was so hot on canning days, the windows steamed up and water trickled down the glass. Mama would have sweat dripping down her brow."

"I guess that's why we ate so many meals at the picnic table Daddy built under the elm tree."

"I didn't much like canning days, because if I was around, she made me take the jars down to the cellar under David's room." I hated the cellar because two of the walls were plain dirt instead of plaster. Big black waterbugs and spiders lived there. "But, I'm glad we moved there when we did. All in all, it was a good place to grow up."

## Adams Street
## Early 1950s

Our next-door neighbor sang, "Lu-lu," as she let herself in through our back porch. "You home?"

"Come on in, Marie," Mama called from the kitchen. "I've got a pot of coffee perking."

"Hi," I said with a shy wave, as I passed Marie on the way out the door to walk to elementary school with Chris and David.

Marie, like many of our neighbors, was German, and spoke with an accent. She always called Mama *Lulu* even though Mama's real name was Lola. She came over to coffee klatch most mornings and sometimes brought streusel muffins or other goodies to share with our family. Mama did the same—toting banana bread or coffee cake over to the Schners every few days.

Mama smiled and laughed more often after we moved, and so did Daddy. They invited friends over for meals and played cards. The people we knew got used to coming in through the back porch. Pretty flowers grew along the path to the shed, and Mama brought in bouquets to put on our table.

My brother, sister, and I liked our new place too. No more outhouse. Kids our own ages lived on our block, and we had a big backyard to play in. Daddy hung a swing from the tree close to our back door that was lots better than anything we had in our old yard.

Marie's son, Joey, had a little black-and-white dog with a smushed-in face and big brown eyes. His name was Spooky. I wished he lived at our house, but at least they let me pet him. When we played baseball with Joey, Spooky liked to chase the balls, and when I talked pretty to him, he licked my face and made me giggle.

We bathed in a galvanized aluminum tub on our screened-in porch on Saturday night. Daddy insulated the windows with plastic film every winter, and Mama made white cotton curtains so we had privacy.

After we lived there two years, Daddy installed a shower on the back porch so we didn't have to bathe in a tub he had to drag out the back door to empty.

I overheard Mama and Daddy chatting one Saturday night on the porch. "Marie came over this morning when you were down in the shed, and we got to talking." Mama paused before she continued. "Marie asked me why we didn't go to church. I didn't have a good answer." Her voice was whiny. "We need to start going to church, Bob —that's what proper folks do."

"Not now, Lola. I got lots of other things to think about."

"We should set a good example for the kids." Mama had been baptized when she was a teenager and liked church. Then my grandpa forbade her and her sisters to go. I'd heard her say once that Grandpa called the church people "self-righteous" and "nosy" to their faces when they came around to invite her family to services. She'd been mortified.

"Maybe later," Daddy said. "I'm plum worn out when the weekend comes. It's the only time I got to relax."

Daddy usually did what Mama wanted, but he could be stubborn too, and she knew when to back off. Maybe that's why she was acting so sour.

I'd heard people talk about church before, but I had never been inside one. I wondered what it was like.

"It would just be Sunday mornings, and I don't see you relaxing that much, anyway. You're always down in the shed on the weekend, fiddling with something."

"When else can I fix stuff 'round here? I ain't had time to overhaul the engine in the Plymouth, and it's knocking bad. And the roof. It has a couple places that needs patching." His voice rose. "You want a roof that doesn't leak, don't you?"

"I want a respectable family." She sounded miffed. "Proper folks go to church on Sundays."

"We'll see," Daddy said, but his tone said otherwise. "Right now I got work to do. Call me when dinner's ready."

I looked out my bedroom window. He was walking down to the shed. That's where he always went when Mama was bugging him.

Mama mumbled as she cooked supper. "He's got plenty of time to do what he wants. Half what he does isn't even his own work. Bet he's down there now fixing something for someone else."

I didn't care if we went to church or not, but I didn't like it when Mama and Daddy argued. I thought about what Mama said. I tried to be respectable like she wanted, but I wasn't sure how going somewhere on Sundays made people that way.

When I asked David what he thought church was like, he said, "My friend Johnny told me they dress people in white bathrobes at his church and dunk them in water—right in front of everybody."

It was all very confusing.

One afternoon when I was eight, I smelled bacon frying, and came into the kitchen. It was sizzling in a skillet so Mama could use the grease to make liver and onions, one of Daddy's favorites. I didn't like liver, but I loved bacon, and Mama let me eat that instead.

Daddy came home from work and gave Mama a kiss like he always did. "I'm going to bed, Lola." He took off the denim cap he always wore. "I'm so worn out I don't know how I got through the last couple of hours."

Mama tilted her head. "Before you even have supper?"

"Save me something. Maybe if I rest a couple hours, I'll feel better. Right now I just got to lie down."

She wrinkled her brow. "You've been awful tired the last few weeks. Something is wrong, Bob."

"I'm okay, Lola, just tired."

I didn't worry because Daddy said he was okay, but that wasn't the last time he rested in bed before supper. He acted exhausted all the time, but he went to work every day.

One evening soon after, Daddy sat us down and said, "Kids, I have to go to a hospital in St. Louis for a while. Help your mother out as much as you can while I'm gone."

"How long will you be gone, Daddy?" I asked.

"I'm not sure."

"Are you bad sick?" Chris asked.

"No, no… and you mustn't worry. Everything will be fine."

"How come you going so far away?" David asked. "Can't you go to Blessing Hospital here in Quincy?"

"The doctors who know how to make me well are down in St. Louis."

The next day when we came home from school, Mama told us Daddy was at Barnes Hospital over a hundred miles away.

Daddy's mother came on the train from Iowa for a

while to help Mama out.

"Land sakes alive," she said when she saw Chris. "With that round face and big brown eyes, you look so much like your daddy." She was nice to all us kids, but she specially liked my sister, and nicknamed her Pistol.

One evening, a month after Grandma Ivy arrived, she came home with three bottles of beer in a paper bag. Mama disapproved of Grandma visiting the tavern on the corner, and Grandma thought Mama was too strict with us kids. They didn't argue, but I could tell from the looks that passed between them and the snide remarks that they didn't like each other.

Grandma mumbled under her breath as she put the bottles in our refrigerator. Mama's mouth was in a tight line when she brought in a laundry basket of towels and sheets from the clothesline. She snapped a pillow slip and folded it, looking real mad.

The next day, a taxicab parked outside our house, and Grandma got in with her suitcase and left. She didn't come back. I felt bad because I liked Grandma Ivy; she did some of our chores and always took up for us. Mama was happier with her gone, though, so she didn't fuss at us as much.

With Daddy gone, and now Grandma. Mama

needed help. She gave us more chores to do. Chris and I took turns washing and drying the dishes. David, taller and stronger than us girls, took the garbage down to the trash cans at the alley and brought fuel oil up from the shed for the stove when Mama needed it.

Marie was over a lot more often, and we stayed next door with her when Mama had to take the bus somewhere.

"I miss Daddy," I told Mama one evening. He wasn't much of a hugger, but life wasn't right without him.

"I miss him, too," she said, "but we'll be okay until he comes home."

"When will that be?" I asked.

"Just a little longer. Daddy's doing fine, though. Don't worry."

I took her at her word—and I didn't worry. Even though I wasn't afraid for Daddy, I tried not to think about him because it made me sad that he was far away. I wanted him to come home so bad I felt hollow inside. Every few days, I asked Mama when he was coming home. She always said the same thing. "Just a little longer."

I never doubted what Mama said until my teacher at school questioned me about how my dad was.

"He's fine," I told her. But I started to wonder if maybe Daddy wasn't so fine. No teacher had ever inquired about the health of one of my parents before.

When I asked David, he said, "Daddy must be really sick." He brushed a shock of brown hair from his earnest eyes. "Don't tell Chris. She still believes what Mama says—that Daddy is fine."

St. Louis was 140 miles downriver, and Mama didn't drive. She'd taken a train twice to visit Daddy while we stayed at our Aunt Emma's house. We only got to visit him once. I'd never been on a train before.

I loved the clickety-clack sound as we rolled along the tracks. We took turns sitting by the window to watch the blur of trees, houses, and farmland rush by. The man who came by to collect our tickets looked a little like Daddy and was friendly to us kids. Mama sat quietly staring at the seat in front of her.

We stayed overnight in what she called a boarding house and walked to the hospital. Chris slept in a bed with Mama, and David and I shared the other bed in the little room. I didn't like sleeping in a stranger's house. There were noises I wasn't used to, and the blankets were scratchy.

We got to see Daddy for only a few minutes. I was

excited about seeing him, but the hospital was so different from any place I'd been. Lights flickered over a long gray hallway lined with doors where people dressed in white came and went—and it smelled bad. Daddy didn't look like himself. He was pale and seemed smaller. Plus, he wore something that looked more like an apron than jammies—baby-blue with little pink flowers all over it.

But he sounded the same. "I'm getting a lot better," he told us. "I'll be coming home soon."

Soon didn't come for another month.

# April, 2019, Saturday Morning

"Did it ever hit you," I ask as we sit in Chris's car in the alley, "how close Daddy came to dying when we were little?"

"Not really— not when I was a kid. I guess for a while they weren't sure he'd make it, and we never knew." She shakes her head and sighs. "I didn't even know he was sick until he went to St. Louis. You would have thought we'd figure out how serious it was. I mean he was in the hospital for a long time."

"I think Mama did a lot of pretending because she didn't want to worry us."

We kid had been oblivious to his fever and chills, and the night sweats and shortness of breath that sent him to a doctor. We didn't find out until much later that he had a serious infection of the lining of his heart—*subacute bacterial endocarditis*—or that the doctors said he'd die if they didn't get the infection under control.

"I think Barnes Hospital must have been one of the few places they were conducting trials with penicillin," I say. "Thank God for penicillin."

"Amen!"

I gaze at the yard and the back of our old house. I couldn't imagine it without our father.

Chris points at the massive stump about halfway up the long narrow backyard. "It doesn't look right without the huge river birch Daddy transplanted from the bottoms? That was a great tree."

"I wonder if Daddy knew they cut it down."

"Probably," Chris says. "Unless he died before the tree."

"Could be. Remember how Daddy used to wheeze when he exerted himself?" I meet Chris's eyes. "He worked just as hard when he got home from the hospital as he did before—and that was with damaged heart valves. The doctors told him to slow down."

"I don't think it was in his nature to slow down," Chris says. "He always had to be doing something. I think he felt lucky Moorman's kept his job for him."

"They would have been hard pressed to find someone better at repairing machinery at the factory." I take a picture of the yard. "That's why he was on call like a doctor. Remember the time they called just before we were leaving for vacation and he had to go into work?"

"It's a good thing they didn't have cell phones back then. At least they couldn't call him to come in after we left."

I laugh. "Yeah. The good ole days."

We don't talk for a few minutes. The old elm tree close to the back door has been replaced by what looks like an oak, and big enough to have been there for many years. There's no swing hanging from its branches and no picnic table in its shade. No flowers along the walkway and no vegetable garden either. I wonder if we would have been able to stay in the house if our dad had died. Mama didn't work and didn't even drive.

"I shudder to think how our lives would've changed if Daddy had died," I say.

Chris nods. "It all seems inevitable now, but our childhood could have been very different."

"Our lives did change though. I'm sure almost dying did it. Family became a lot more important to Daddy."

"I guess that was about the time he got that little motorboat and we started going to the river more often."

I glance at the weathered shed where Daddy spent so much time fixing things. "That old shed didn't see as much of him on weekends after that." My mind goes back to all the things our family did together—exploring the Mississippi, swimming, and fishing. Our other outings, too—hiking and picnicking in the woods, mushroom hunting in the spring and gathering nuts in the fall. We had a rich childhood, thanks to that protracted illness that changed Daddy's priorities.

"You know, the day my Kelly graduated from high school," I say, "Daddy told me he had prayed in the hospital that he'd live long enough to see us kids grown, never dreaming he'd get to see his grandkids grow up."

"I never heard him talk about it," Chris says, "but I knew our lives changed for the better. That was when we started going to church too."

"Every Sunday and Wednesday." I smile. "Mama finally had her respectable family."


As Chris and I sit in her car in the alley behind our old house, a neighbor comes out and ties a dog to her clothesline. The dog spots us when the woman goes inside and it begins to bark, straining against the rope holding it.

"I'm glad he's tied up." Chris nods toward the dog. "He looks mean."

"You know, when I was little, someone told me that animals would never hurt you if you weren't frightened and meant them no harm. And I believed it."

Chris shakes her head with an amused expression. "I guess that would make you extremely brave… until you ran into an animal that didn't care if you were afraid or not."

"It's not like I had much opportunity to test the theory with anything but domestic animals." Cats and dogs were about the only animals we saw regularly—maybe a horse now and then. "But you're right. It made me incredibly brave." I glance at her. "Do you remember Mr. Ziegler's horse?"

"Mr. Ziegler?"

"The iceman. You know—a big burly man with a round nose—friendly and wore a leather apron. Remember? He carried big tongs to pick up the blocks of ice when he delivered it? That was the late forties, when we first moved to Adams Street. His horse's name was Sally."

"I sort of remember the horse. Black as night?"

"Right. We only saw them a year or so because

Daddy bought a used refrigerator after that, and we didn't need the ice. Anyway, sometimes Mr. Ziegler let me feed Sally a piece of apple. I had to've been only about six, but he showed me how to stretch my fingers really wide with the apple in my palm so she could pluck the treat. She had the biggest yellow teeth I ever saw. Then Sally put her head down low so I could stroke her nose. It was so soft."

"I'm not sure I was brave enough to try that."

"You were only five"—I give her a wry grin —"and you didn't know the secret was to not be afraid."

A movement catches my eye through the window of the screened-in back porch of our old house. "Someone's checking us out."

"We probably better get out of here before they suspect something nefarious," Chris says.

"From two old ladies?" I laugh. "It's just as well; I want to get to the park while we still have the morning light."

"The park it is." Chris starts the engine and we drive down the alley and turn east on Adams.

I point at a house a couple blocks down from our old place. "Remember when Aunt Emma lived there?"

"I'd almost forgotten," Chris says. "They moved farther north when we were fairly young. I do remember that mean dog that lived a couple houses from them."

"Yep, me too. But I wasn't afraid of him."

Chris snickers. "Of course, you weren't."

## Animals
## Early 1950s

The summer after Daddy came home from the hospital, our family drove two hundred miles from Illinois to Iowa to visit relatives. I had never been on a real farm, and we were going to stay a whole week in the country at his sister's place. I could hardly contain my excitement at the idea of seeing the animals up close, maybe even petting them.

Green fields of corn lined the road with tassels waving in the breeze. A red barn and white house stood in the distance flanked by a row of trees on either side.

"This has to be the place," Daddy said, turning into the long gravel drive.

I stared at the peaceful scene in wonder as we rumbled toward the house with a wide porch—an honest-to-goodness farm. A brown dog barked at us when we got close. We parked on the gravel next to a weathered shed, and I opened the car door first, eager to pet him. I held out my hand for him to smell, and he wagged his tail and sniffed it, then greeted me like I was an old friend. Everyone else got out of the car as I petted him.

"He's friendly," I said. "I wish we had a dog just like him."

Aunt Martha, whom I had met only once, came out on the porch, smiling as she wiped her hands on the bib apron covering her round middle. She spread out her arms and hugged us all one at a time. "It's been a coon's age." She put her hand on David's shoulder, who at nine, was already taller than she was. "And just look how the youngin's have grown."

The farm was paradise. Outside it smelled of hay and honeysuckle, and inside, always something delicious—bread baking, cookies fresh from the oven, bacon frying. David, Chris, and I played hide-and-seek in the cornfield with our cousins, and in the barn loft, giggling as we told stories. David was good at telling scary tales that made our cousins squirm.

Best of all were the animals. Cows, pigs and goats. Uncle Wilber lifted me up onto a horse and led it around while I held on tight. I fed pears and carrots to goats, and I even touched a pig's back through the fence. It snorted at me, and my uncle said, "Watch your fingers, child. That one bites." I pulled my hand back even though I was sure the pig was just saying hello.

Chickens lived on the farm, too—lots of them. After breakfast the first morning, Aunt Martha asked us kids, "Who wants to help me gather eggs?"

My hand shot up. "I do. I do."

She handed me a basket to put over my arm as we went into the chicken yard. Fat gold and white hens, and some smaller gold-and-black ones gathered around us.

"Those little dark ones are banties," she said, throwing some table scraps to them. Two or three fancy roosters with greenish tail feathers strutted among them.

When we entered the chicken coop the sweet, musty, smell of hay tickled my nose. "Don't try to get the eggs from the boxes with chickens sitting in them. I'll get those."

I carefully picked up the warm eggs from the unattended boxes, delighted to be taking part. Sometimes a hen in one of the boxes didn't like Aunt Martha taking her egg and squawked, flapping her wings.

"She's broody," my aunt said. "She wants to sit on her egg until it hatches."

I felt sorry for the hens when Aunt Martha shoved them off the hay nests. They wouldn't get to hatch their baby chicks.

The eggs were not like the white ones Mama bought at the grocery store. Some were brown, and a few were greenish, but they all tasted the same when my aunt made eggs and sausage with hot biscuits for breakfast.

That afternoon, Aunt Martha let the chickens out of the fenced-in area around the coop to peck around for bugs while my oldest cousin cleaned their home. Incredibly, one of the fat, honey-colored hens let me pick her up and carry her around as I petted her smooth feathers. I named her Mimi after a girl at school with strawberry-blonde hair. Everyone was amazed, but not me. Why would Mimi be afraid of me? I had nothing but good intentions toward her.

I'd had just enough experience with animals that I trusted they would never harm me. I touched, petted, and cuddled any critter who let me get close.

Cautionary tales from adults didn't shake my conviction. If an animal harmed someone, I was certain it was because they were scared. I wasn't.

One summer afternoon, I was returning from our

cousin's house where we'd been playing hide-and-seek. Phillip, the same age as me, lived on the same street, just two blocks east from us, and I was walking home alone. A dozen or so cement steps led up a high bank to the houses and front yards on that part of Adams. A German shepherd lived on their block. He was seldom outside unattended, but on one occasion he had bitten my Aunt Emma.

"When you go home," my aunt had warned me, "take the long way around. You don't want to run into that mean dog."

I was tired from playing with Phillip, though, and that route around the block would have taken me twice as long to walk.

It didn't matter if that German shepherd was outside; I had nothing to worry about. He would know I wasn't afraid of him.

As I passed the place where he lived, I heard a dog barking up on the steep bank. He came running down the hill toward me with his white teeth bared.

I stopped, stood my ground and faced him, unafraid.

The shepherd stopped short a few feet from me and growled.

I frowned and shook a finger at the dog. "You

naughty, naughty dog, acting ugly and trying to scare people."

He looked at me for a few moments, then retreated up to the yard.

That experience made me even more fearless. Many times after, I recounted the anecdote as proof that my belief was more than theory.

My affection for animals was mostly for warm-blooded mammals and birds. But, except for insects, my bravery and goodwill extended to all of God's creatures—even snakes. That was no doubt because my brother kept snakes in a big cage on the screened-in back porch.

"I want to hold him," I said to David when he was handling his kingsnake once. The docile reptile was striking with bands of red, yellow, and black.

"Don't drop him," he said, handing the snake to me.

The colorful scales were dry and smooth as the snake wound its body around my arm, and stuck his head between the buttons on my blouse.

"What's he doing that for?" I wiggled as the snake continued to slither under my clothes, tickling my ribs.

"It's warm in there. He likes that." David chuckled. "They're cold-blooded, you know."

I realize now how tolerant our parents were of such things, but it seemed natural then. They drew the line at poisonous species. Twice my brother's snakes went missing. The first time several water snakes escaped and were later found curled together in our cellar under the water heater. The other time David's boa constrictor crawled out from under the refrigerator during supper.

At nine, I became a Girl Scout, and my parents let me go to a week-long day camp. Our leader taught us about outdoor etiquette like leaving things the way we found them and fire safety. We practiced knots, learned about wildlife, swam in the creek, and explored the woods with our counselor. I liked it because at night we returned home to sleep in our own beds.

When the Girl Scout counselor told us about snakes—what kinds lived in our area, their habits and what they looked like—I felt rather smug. I'd been with my brother when he caught his corn snake and I'd handled his kingsnake too. When she asked if any of us knew the venomous snakes that lived in Illinois, I was quick to answer.

"There's only three kinds. Water moccasins,

rattlesnakes, and copperheads," I said, proudly. "They're all pit vipers."

"Very good, Alice." Our counselor smiled at me. She showed us all pictures of the poisonous snakes in our area—all with triangular-shaped heads and thick bodies.

Some of the girls winced when they looked at the pictures.

I already knew what they looked like. Anyone around my brother learned about snakes. "Those are rare. Most snakes are harmless, and you don't have to be scared of them," I said. "They won't hurt you if you're not afraid."

Their faces told me no one believed my assertion.

Later that afternoon, some of us were wading in the little creek that flowed through the campground. A girl screamed and pointed to a snake swimming up stream. It wasn't much longer than a foot. "A cottonmouth water moccasin!" She splashed as she hurried from the water

A counselor came running.

"No, it's not," I said. "It's just a water snake." I headed toward the snake and grabbed its middle. It bit me three times before I could let it go. The bites felt like pinpricks.

I trudged out of the water—shocked that it had bitten me. I wasn't going to hurt the snake. I just wanted to show everyone that the snake wasn't a moccasin. Truth be told, I was showing off.

A big commotion ensued. Several girls had witnessed the incident and described it with big eyes and earnest voices to the adults who gathered around me. They all looked concerned.

Embarrassed and irritated, I assured everyone, "It wasn't poisonous—just a little water snake, and it didn't hardly hurt."

The counselor who had come running confirmed that it hadn't looked like a water moccasin, though the snake was long gone. But they were taking no chances. The camp nurse washed the tiny holes with alcohol and squeezed a little blood from the wounds.

"Someone's gone to call your mother to come get you," one counselor said. "How do you feel?"

"Fine! It wasn't poisonous!" I repeated. I wished they hadn't called Mama. She wasn't going to be happy. Mama didn't drive and would have to ask a neighbor to bring her.

The nurse hovered while we waited for my mother, and she watched me carefully for swelling, asking me repeatedly how I felt. By the time Mama arrived, it was obvious I wasn't dying. The neighbor who drove her took us to a clinic, and I got a tetanus shot. Mama scolded me for upsetting everyone.

## April, 2019, Saturday Morning

"I was mad," I tell Chris, grinning. "That stupid snake didn't know the rules."

Chris chuckles as she turns right on Twelfth Street. "You were a piece of work."

We enter South Park, where we'd whiled away so many hours as children. Back then, we'd walked to the park from our house a half mile away.

Chris pulls to a stop along the curb of the upper loop, the well-maintained part of the 135-acre city park. We get out and stroll around. It looks the same, and I find that reassuring in a world that has changed so dramatically. Dozens of huge trees cast shadows across the spacious lawn. Their leaves, not yet in full flower, appear golden and lacy against the sky.

"I think April must be about the prettiest time of year." I snap a photo with my phone.

"Gosh, we had a lot of picnics here," Chris says as we walk past the hundred-year-old pavilion, the site of countless events—church gatherings and wiener roasts, extended family potlucks, and the annual all-afternoon affair hosted by Moorman's, the company where our dad worked. "They all sort of blend together in my mind now."

"It's no wonder. There were so many." I scan the expanse of grass in mottled shades of spring green. "Remember the year you and I won the three-legged race at the Morman's picnic?"

"Mostly I remember the free ice cream any time we wanted it. I loved those picnics."

"I did too." I can still see it so clearly. How could that have been over sixty years ago? The park had teemed with people, eating fried chicken, playing bingo at long tables, and pitching horseshoes.

Chris and I are the only people around now, except for a man with his dog a hundred feet away. The golden retriever barks and jumps at a squirrel scrambling up a tree as his master tries to divert his attention with a Frisbee.

I point to a brick gazebo as we walk back to the car. "I wonder if they still have Sunday concerts in the park." In my mind I can hear a brassy Sousa march and picture families sitting around the bandstand in lawn chairs and on quilts spread on the grass.

"I hope they do. But I have a feeling the younger

generations would consider that sort of thing too old-fashioned."

"Like pitching horseshoes," I say.

Chris raises her brows when we get to the car. "The creek next?"

"Yeah." I smile. "I'm anxious to see it again."

We drive along a winding road, past the hill where we rode our sleds after deep winter snows. "That was a great place for sledding," I say, nodding toward it. "Remember the time Dave slid so fast down that slope, he ended up breaking the ice in the creek?"

"I think he was rather proud of himself—in a frozen, teeth-chattering sort of way." Chris laughs.

I'm floating in warm-hued memories as Chris pulls along the curb at the lower part of the park, our usual destination as kids.

We get out and meander along the side of the road that runs parallel to the creek several feet below. I peer down between trees at the clear water gurgling over rocks the way it had when we were young. A lump forms in my throat as I contemplate my transitory relationship to this creek. Chances are, I will never see it again, but its waters will keep flowing long after I am forgotten.

"Let's climb down and walk along the creek." I point to a break in the trees along the shoulder of the roadway where the land drops off abruptly past the trees to the level of the stream.

"I don't know, Alice. Looks awful steep."

"It's just a few feet." I repeat the mantra of the day. "This could be the last time."

She eyes me warily. "You know we will have to climb back up, too. And I have a few more pounds to haul up than you. Gravity will be working against us."

I laugh. "Where's that adventurous sister of mine? We've done it a million times. I'll go first." I hold on to saplings to steady myself as I descend to the rocky creek bank, sliding down the last two feet, but land upright.

I brush dirt off the back of my jeans and look up at my sister. She frowns and turns to face the cliff, grabbing branches as she climbs backwards down the hill.

"I won't let you fall," I say as I reach up and push against her to support her in case her foot slips.

We walk for a while along the timeless stream. I stop, kneel on the rocky bank, and dip my hand into the cool water—into my childhood. I'm eight years old again, gazing down at the rippling water and the mossy stones a few inches under the surface. These waters hold so many memories—catching crawdads and minnows, wading in the shallows.

"Hey Chris." I look up and grin at her from the hard limestone bank. "Roll up your pant legs and wade in like we did as kids so I can take your picture for Facebook."

"Very funny! Are you going to come in after me when I slip and fall on my keister?"

I smirk. "Somehow I didn't think you'd go for it."

Chris holds out her hand to pull me back to my feet, and we wander farther along the creek. We both snap a few photos.

"Remember pretending we were explorers when we hiked along here—and that trail up there?" I point to the natural shelf about twenty feet up the cliff on the opposite side of the creek. A treacherous path, just inches from the face of the steep cliff, follows the waterway for about fifty yards. "The drop seemed farther when we were kids, didn't it?" To keep kids from taking the narrow trail, parents told the story of a kid falling to his death from it. The warnings only fueled challenges.

Chris looks up and shakes her head. "It's a wonder

we survived our childhoods. Mama would've had a fit if she'd known."

A cardinal trills and a flash of red catches my eye in the branches above. In the distance, I hear the songs of dozens of birds calling to one another in the trees. I inhale a deep satisfying breath. It is all so familiar. It seems like we spent as much time at the park as we did in our own backyard, but it's probably a trick of memory.

When it's time to climb back up to the road, Chris says, "I'll go first this time so you can push me."

I stand behind Chris pushing on her rump with all the power I can muster as she grabs hold of exposed tree roots and branches to pull herself up. I'm panting by the time she is safely atop the earthen cliff.

"Your turn," she says breathing hard as she looks down at me.

I get halfway up and stall. "I don't think I can make it." I didn't expect this problem. I'm healthy and not overweight, but without someone behind me pushing, I don't have the strength to pull myself up even holding on to a tree sapling.

My sister bends over and extends her hand. "Grab hold and I'll pull."

"What if I pull you down instead?" I suspect that

would be the case. Chris is an old woman too. My pulse speeds up, and I'm getting hot. How do I get myself in situations like this? Intellectually I know my body is winding down. What does one expect at seventy-six? Yet, it is hard to accept emotionally that I can't do what I did in my prime.

"Well, there's no one else around," Chris says. "If we can't both get up here under our own steam, it's not going to happen."

I imagine the humiliation of calling 911 because we hadn't acted our age.

Chris looks around at our immediate surroundings and lays her hand on the trunk of a mature tree growing beside her. With her weight against the back of the tree, she reaches toward me. "If you can get just a little higher, we'll have the tree to support me. It's not going anywhere."

I clutch a tree root with one hand and the sapling with the other and heave, pulling myself up another few inches, finding purchase for my foot on a protruding rock. I quickly grasp her hand and with a herculean effort, she pulls me the rest of the way up.

We stand looking down, panting. It had been so easy when we were kids.

"The last time, for sure," I say, my legs trembling

from the exertion.

We drive to the park's spring last. The water that bubbles up from somewhere in the earth feeds two small lakes. Trees line the far side of both lakes, and a walkway borders this side. The chartreuse leaves on the trees create a lovely contrast with the darker evergreens.

Chris points a few feet from the spring. "Look. Is that duck sitting on a nest?"

A white duck is resting on a mound of sticks and brown grass under the low-hanging branches of a blooming redbud tree. She is the picture of indifference while her mate, with black markings, watches us with a wary stance.

"You have nothing to be concerned about, daddy duck." I crouch down and take a photo, framing them both with the purple redbud branches.

Water gurgles nearby as we walk on. The spring still fascinates me. When I was a kid, the idea that water ran underground intrigued me.

We stare at the little pool created by the water spilling from under a rocky ledge. Out of the blue, Chris says, "Did I ever tell you about the man who exposed himself to me here?"

"What?" I'm incredulous. "You're kidding. Why have you never mentioned that? I mean, that's disturbing."

"Well, you never told me about the baby mice. That was a lot more disturbing."

She has a point. "But I see you almost every day. I don't know how that never came up."

"Not much to tell. You may have even been with me. We usually went to the park together."

I chuckle. "I think I would have remembered that."

"Anyway, I was down here at the spring—looking in the water and this man comes up and starts talking to me."

"How old was he?"

"Who knows? At the time I thought he was old, but then I was just a kid,  so…"

"Did you talk with him?"

"I may have told him my name if he asked, but I didn't say much."

I gave her a look, tilting my head. Chris was always the friendly one, and I'm not sure she is remembering right. I've seen her talk a blue streak to total strangers many times.

"Really, I didn't!"

"What happened? What did he do?"

"I didn't see him do anything. I mean, all of a sudden there it was—this long thing hanging out of his pants. I wasn't even sure what it was. I mean, what did I know at that age? I'd never seen a guy naked."

"Oh, my goodness." I suppress a giggle. "What did you do?"

"I ran home."

"Did you tell Mama?"

"Heavens, no. I wouldn't have had the words to tell her, and there wasn't anything to do about it, anyway. I was probably afraid Mama wouldn't let us go to the park anymore if she knew."

I sigh. "That would have been a shame. Just think of all the fun we would have missed."


We leave the park and drive the half mile back to Adams Street. Chris swings around the block past the houses on our street again, pointing out the places our old neighbors lived. "That's the Schneider's, of course, and the Steffin's there." She gestures to a house about a block away from ours.

"Mary Lou Gronert lived there." She calls the names of at least seven more.

"I'm amazed you still remember all that," I say. "I couldn't begin to name so many."

Chris grins. "I got around more than you did."

"You were a regular social butterfly, as I recall."

Unlike my sister, I was shy, and preferred blending into the background—even at home. The lively discussions during family dinners were mostly exchanges between my father and David. I had my own ideas, but it was rarely worth the effort to voice them. My sister, however, wasn't dissuaded by their banter.

Pistol, the nickname our grandmother gave Chris was fitting. She was full of unreserved enthusiasm. Though the years have tempered her energies and impulsiveness, she is still more outgoing than I am.

Family photographs of us as children almost always show me frowning and my sister wearing a big smile. Mama often dressed us alike, even though we couldn't have been more different. For years, we wore the same size, and people sometimes asked if we were twins.

Chris was born fifteen months after me—an "accident" Daddy once revealed. Mama was aghast when he let it slip, saying, "Bob, you're going to warp that child."

That would have been difficult to do. Chris was as happy and gregarious as children get.

"I'll never forget your sixth birthday—the summer after we moved to Adams Street," I say.

She laughs. "Ah, yes. The party."

## Party
## Early 1950s

"What do you want tomorrow for your birthday supper, Chris?" Mama asked at breakfast.

"Barbecue ribs." Chris didn't hesitate. She'd chosen ribs anytime Mama gave her a choice.

Birthdays were strictly family occasions for us. Mama would make a cake and whatever the birthday child wanted for supper. We'd eat our meal—just the five of us—blow out candles, and eat the cake. There would be a present from Mama and Daddy. Simple family celebrations.

The day before Chris's birthday was hot and muggy, even for July. I stayed inside and drew pictures with the window exhaust fan supplying a constant breeze. Dave was reading in his room, and Chris was outside somewhere—probably playing baseball with Joey, the boy who lived next door.

The phone rang that afternoon. I heard Mama say to the caller, "Well, uh. Let's see… about 1:30." She sounded flustered. "Yes, absolutely, we'd love for all of you to come, but please, there's no need to bring a present. It will just be a simple little get-together to celebrate."

She hung up and said, "What on earth has that child done?"

Curious, I went into the kitchen. Mama sat in a chair by the phone just staring at the floor, looking pale.

"What's wrong, Mama?" I asked.

"Your sister invited the Gronerts over for her birthday. The whole family." She shook her head. "We hardly know Mary Lou's parents, and they are expecting a party here—tomorrow!"

She went to the back door and yelled outside. "Christine Lee?" She called three more times, but Chris didn't respond. "Of all people, why the Gronerts?" Mama returned to the kitchen and stopped dead in her tracks. Her eyes widened. "How many other people did she invite?" She covered her mouth. "Oh, no!"

The question was partially answered throughout the afternoon, as more neighbors called to confirm the time of Chris's birthday party. Mama was busy in the hot kitchen making Chris's cake and mixing up an extra one, groaning every time the phone rang. "Yes, yes, come at 1:30. No gifts," she said in a cheery voice. "We'll just have cake and visit while the children play. Of course, we'd love to have you come."

Another call came as she pulled the second cake out of the oven, the sweet, chocolate scent filling the house. After assuring the caller her family was indeed welcome, Mama sent David with our Radio Flyer wagon to the grocery store two blocks away to buy more flour, sugar, and Crisco.

Chris returned home late in the afternoon, and I expected Mama to be angry at her, but she didn't act like she was mad. "I hear you've invited the neighbors to a party tomorrow. What in heaven's name gave you the idea to do that?"

Bouncing on her toes, Chris beamed. "I decided to have a birthday party like Norma Myers did." Norma was a girl in Chris's kindergarten class. "It will be fun."

"Tell me who you invited? *Everyone* you invited." I was amazed Mama was being so nice to Chris. "I have to know how many cakes to make."

"Everybody on our block, but Mrs. Steffen wasn't home. I can go over and ask her after supper. I don't want to hurt her feelings. I invited Glenda and Rosemary Becker over on Eighth Street too."

"Anybody else?"

Chris screwed up her face and thought. "Oh, yeah, and the Hubers."

Two cakes were cooling on the counter when Daddy came home from the factory, and a third was in the oven. Mama must have told Daddy, but they didn't talk about it during supper, and Daddy seemed the same as always.

Saturday morning, he and Mama were busy getting things ready for Chris's birthday party. Our neighbor, Marie, came over to help Mama frost the cakes and make punch. She also loaned us all her kitchen and lawn chairs. Daddy cut the grass and set up the chairs and folding tables in the backyard. When he finished, he went to the store for ice cream, paper plates, plastic utensils, and balloons.

Chris sparkled with excitement when the guests started arriving. Mama and Daddy greeted everyone like they'd been anticipating the party for weeks and were thrilled to see everyone. Neighborhood kids ran around the backyard, playing red rover and jumping rope while adults sat around talking and laughing. After Chris blew out her candles, we all had ice cream and cake— chocolate, banana, and coconut. At least twenty people came, and everyone seemed to have fun. I don't think anybody but Marie and our family ever knew that Chris hadn't had our parents' permission for the party.

# April, 2019, Saturday Morning

Chris smiles at me, then looks back at the street as we make another circuit around our old neighborhood. "It never dawned on me at the time that I was making a problem for Mama and Daddy. I just thought all I had to do was invite people, and I'd have a party like Norma Myers."

I laugh. "It worked. If you had asked our parents ahead of time, I'm sure they would have told you no."

"No doubt"—she laughs—"but they couldn't very well un-invite people."

"They must have really hustled to put together that party. But they did somehow. I think Mama made at least three cakes, maybe more. They may not have planned the party, but I think they did their best to make it a special birthday for you."

Chris nods. "It *was* a great party."

"I remember Daddy dipping ice cream from that huge container. That was the first time I'd seen dry ice. The smoke fascinated me." I shake my head, chuckling again. "I think half the neighborhood must have shown up."

Chris grins. "Not just kids either."

"Well, it's a great story. It's just so… you." I take a photo of our block with the limbs of large trees arching over the street. I glance at Chris as she drives. "Did Mama or Daddy ever scold you about it? I'm sure throwing a party wasn't in their budget."

"I don't remember them being mad. You'd think they would be, but maybe they didn't want to spoil my birthday. Mama did set me down and made it clear I was never to pull a stunt like that again." She laughs. "I did get the message. I'm sure you noticed that our birthday parties after that were just the five of us again."

I check the time. "If we're going to take showers before the open house for David, we better head back to the hotel. After crawling up that hill in the park, I absolutely need to."

I think about the party as we drive north again, and the lack of them after that day. Somehow I never felt cheated. We've laughed about Chris's party for years. It just epitomized my sister so well. "We may not have had parties," I say, "but we never lacked for adventure—picking blackberries, picnicking, and fishing—all things that didn't cost money."

"Mushroom hunting," Chris adds, "and don't forget gathering pecans and walnuts in the fall. We got to do more than the families of my friends. I even felt sorry for them."

"Mama and Daddy didn't have a lot of money. It wasn't about buying us things; For them, it was about giving us experiences."

## Pecans
## Early 1950s

Chris squirmed as Mama buttoned up her sweater and pulled it down over the long pants she insisted we wear. "You don't want to get cold, do you?"

"Where we going?" I asked, buttoning my matching sweater.

"An outing into the woods." A smile shone in Mama's light blue eyes. "And if things go well, I'll make us a pie in the morning."

"What kind of pie?" Chris asked. "Custard? I like custard."

"You'll see." Mama turned to me. "Alice, tell David to wear his jacket." Our brother was eleven and way bigger than my sister and me.

"David!" I yelled in the direction of his room, "Mama said to wear your jacket."

Mama rolled her eyes. "Proper children don't scream in the house, Alice." She shooed me away. "Go see if your brother's dressed warm."

I groaned and headed to my brother's room.

A few minutes later, Mama scooted us out the back door into the crisp autumn air. "Go get in the car now. I'll be there in a minute."

When our parents climbed into the car, I asked, "Where we going, Daddy?"

"To the bottoms to get us some pecans." Daddy started the car.

The bottomland along the river, especially along the Missouri side, was fertile farmland. We'd gathered morel mushrooms there the previous spring.

A man our dad knew at the factory had told him where a native pecan tree grew. "It's just waiting for us—full of nuts ready to harvest." Daddy said. "No sense leaving them to the crows and squirrels."

In a few minutes, we crossed the mile-wide river and turned down a gravel country road as Chris and I pressed our noses to the window. After rattling over a wooden bridge spanning a little creek, Daddy slowed the car to a crawl and scrutinized the landscape. He pulled over to the side of the road and we all piled out of the old Plymouth. A hawk screeched above us as it glided in a wide circle. Daddy opened the trunk of the car and pulled out four buckets and a rolled-up blue tarpaulin. He surveyed the field beyond the fence and pointed to the edge of a stand of trees. "It must be in there. Let's go."

Daddy tossed the four buckets over the barbed wire fence, then stepped down on the slack bottom wires and pulled up on the top one while my brother crawled through into the field. Mama helped us girls through the fence. Our parents each took a bucket, gave one to my brother, and a fourth for Chris and me to carry. We swung the bucket between us as we walked the fifty yards or so to the edge of the trees.

We wandered around in the forest for several minutes, smelling damp earth and manure. My sister and I stayed close to Mama. I didn't know what a pecan tree looked like, but I scanned the maze of branches above us, some with yellow or brown leaves and the rest nearly bare with patches of blue sky showing. My mouth watered when I thought of the sweet filling and flakey crust of the pie Mama would make with the nuts. Pecan pie was a rare treat for us.

"Your dad will call us when he finds the tree, so listen for him," Mama said.

I listened hard but heard only the lowing of cattle far in the distance and a crow cawing almost nonstop.

"I bet that crow knows where the pecans are," Mama said.

Chris held up a large feather she'd found. "I got me a good Indian feather." She stuck it in her hair, but it wouldn't stay upright.

I spotted an acorn on the carpet of fallen leaves, picked it up, and showed it to her. "Indians used to eat acorns in the olden days," I said. "Want a bite."

Chris made a face. "You're making that up."

"Nuh-uh. We learned that in school."

"I found it," Daddy hollered, and we all ran through the trees toward his voice. I stumbled on a root in my excitement.

The pecan tree was enormous. Nuts lay on the ground, and more hung from the branches. I reached to pick up a pecan from the forest floor and showed it to Daddy.

"The ones down here are probably bad." He pointed to a small round hole in the shell. "See that? A weevil worm's been in there eating the pecan." He pointed up to the nuts hanging on the branches above us. "We want the ones still up there."

I wondered how we'd get the pecans that hadn't fallen. Mama helped Daddy spread out the tarp on the ground. He climbed up into the tree and out onto one of the big limbs.

"You be careful, Bob," Mama shouted. "Isn't that far enough?" She liked the outdoors as much as Daddy, but she was more cautious.

"Not if we want the pecans." Daddy inched out farther until the branch began to sway under his weight.

Chris stood with her mouth open and eyes wide as she watched.

"Can I climb up in the tree, too, Daddy?" David yelled.

"Not this time, son. I need you on the ground to help your mother," he shouted. "Now stand back." Daddy shook the branch. Pecans, brown husks, and leaves rained down onto the blue tarp.

"Look at all those nuts," Chris said laughing.

We scrambled to collect the pecans and put them in our buckets.

When he'd shaken all the nuts that would fall from one branch and we'd collected them, Daddy moved to a limb on the other side of the tree. My brother helped Mama pull the tarp and spread it out beneath Daddy, and he shook that branch. Soon our buckets were full of pecans.

"I guess we'll leave the rest for the crows," Daddy said and eased back down out of the pecan tree and jumped the last few feet.

"This'll be plenty for my holiday baking," Mama said as Daddy rolled up the tarpaulin. She glanced at me with bright eyes. "And a pie tomorrow."

With our bounty in hand, we started back to the car. The bucket Chris and I carried between us was so heavy with nuts we could hardly manage it.

About twenty feet from the fence, Mama yelled, "Run kids! That bull is coming this way!"

I looked behind me. An enormous black bull was charging across the field toward us. It was closing the distance fast. I gasped, and my stomach flipped.

Daddy grabbed the bucket Chris and I were carrying. "Hurry!"

I seized Chris's hand, and too frightened to look back again, we raced to the car, screaming all the way. Daddy pitched the buckets over the barbed wire fence and practically threw us over too. The hem of my pants caught on the fence and ripped. Mama and David scrambled right behind us. Their pecans joined ours, strewn all over the side of the road.

The angry beast snorted and stopped a few yards

back from the fence. He tramped at the dirt with his front hoof. Heart pounding, I realized the bull had been in the pasture the whole time. I started to shake.

"Breathe," Mama said, putting her arm around me. "Deep breaths. In. Out. That's it." After a few minutes my heart beat normally again.

As we gathered up the nuts spilled in our haste, Mama glared at Daddy, her face red. "Bob, did you know cattle were in there before we went in?"

He grinned. "Exciting, wasn't it?"

# April, 2019, Saturday Noon

Chris pulls into the Holiday Inn parking lot. "I remember that bull too. That fence seemed awfully puny with an angry, thousand-pound bull on the other side. I was glad we never went back to that same pecan tree."

"Mama probably made sure of that." I get out of Chris's car. "It was scary. My heart pounds just thinking about it."

Our father's grin spread across Chris's face. "Daddy was always a bit of a daredevil."

My thoughts shift to David and the memorial open house as we take the elevator to our room, shower, and change our clothes. It's being held at the home of Rose's brother not far from the hotel. In less than an hour, Chris and I park along the curb at their condo. It is neatly landscaped and in a stylish neighborhood with manicured lawns and cheerful flowerbeds.

"This is a lot nicer place than Dave and Rose's,"

Chris says.

Their house in Springfield has peeling paint, more weeds than grass in the yard, and a tavern across the street. Dave had been on disability for the last few years after an injury, but before he retired, he'd been a zookeeper, and had worked with elephants for years. Rose was a practical nurse. They could have afforded better, yet their place is shabbier than the little house on Adams is now.

We sit in the car for a few minutes before getting out. "I can't help but wonder how Roses' family viewed David," I say. "Do you think they thought of him as a failure? That she could have done better?"

"Maybe." Chris drops her car fob in her purse. "I mean, he *could* have done as well as any of us. It's not like he wasn't intelligent, and they didn't have any kids to raise and educate."

Chris and her husband had been paid well in the corporate world. I'd done well as an artist, and my husband is a retired college professor. When Chris became a widow fourteen years ago, she moved to Oklahoma and built a lovely home in our comfortable neighborhood.

We get out of the car and start walking up the driveway. Chris says, "Somehow it doesn't seem fair we have so much more than he and Rose did."

I've always been a little uncomfortable, too, with the difference in the level of ease my sister and I enjoy and the lifestyle of Dave and Rose. "He made his own choices, Chris. He had his priorities."

"I know. And to his credit, he never seemed bitter or envious."

We walk up the steps to the front porch and ring the bell. Chris brushes a white hair off the shoulder of my navy blouse as we wait. I raise my brows to acknowledge her gesture. Rose answers the door and ushers us in. "Thanks for coming." She attempts a smile, but sorrow shows in her eyes.

"Wouldn't have missed it." We hug. "I'm glad you waited until April."

Rose is gaunt and paler than when I'd seen her last Spring. Her thin, graying hair hugs her neck, and she is wearing a loose-fitting beige dress that brushes her ankles. Rose is the only person there I recognize. I feel ill at ease, even though it's what I'd expected. She introduces us to her family and friends. They are all pleasant and welcoming. I'll be lucky if I remember any of their names. Her sister-in-law directs us to the kitchen bar, where soft drinks and snacks are arranged—sandwich makings, fruit and desserts. "Help yourself," she says.

"Looks delish." I take a small plate and fill it with a variety of finger foods. I look around for Chris and find a place to sit next to her in the living room.

She points to the big-screen TV. "Look." A slide show of family photos is being shown.

"Hey, that's great!" I balance my plate on my knees. "That's the PowerPoint presentation you made and sent to Rose, isn't it?"

"Yes. She tells me a friend of hers added more recent photos of her and Dave."

It seems strange to view pictures from our childhood with a group of strangers who hadn't even known David until he was well into his twenties.

I munch on the refreshments and watch the slides cycle through. A photo comes on of us three kids. I'm in the middle holding our dog, Mike, when he was a puppy. A sudden mix of emotions engulfs me—sadness for sure, and regret. But the acute grief I should feel at my brother's passing seems out of reach. There have been too many years of minimal contact, too many years of living very separate and divergent lives. My mind turns inward, and I don't see the next few slides.

## Mike
## Early 1950s

"Stay away from me!" I shouted at my little sister. Chris was six, and being a pest. I'd already gotten in trouble once today for arguing with her, and I was in a bad mood. And now, the noxious smell of sauerkraut and dumplings Mama was making for supper filled the house.

I liked most of the food she cooked, but sauerkraut tasted… well, sour. At least she didn't make me eat the kraut—just a dumpling. Some kids got a peanut butter or cheese sandwich if they didn't like what their mother served, but ours wasn't that sympathetic. We ate what Mama cooked or did without.

I fled to the screened-in back porch to escape the odor. A June breeze swept through the windows. My father's car pulled in from the alley and parked on the gravel next to the shed.

"Daddy's home!" I hollered into the kitchen.

He strode up the back walk with a big grin,

cradling a shoe box in both hands, holding it close against his chest.

"What's in the box, Daddy?" I asked, opening the door for him as he stepped into the porch. I bounced on my toes.

He grinned wider. "Go get Chris and Dave, and I'll show you."

When I returned with my brother and sister, Mama came out onto the porch too.

Daddy put the box on the floor. The lid moved, and I heard a squeaky sound. I clasped my hands to my chest and held my breath.

My father reached down and lifted off the lid. A puppy looked up and barked an adorable *hello*. Black with white legs, chest, and muzzle, he was the cutest thing I'd ever seen. Instant love.

Daddy picked up the wiggling bundle and put him in my arms. Warmth radiated through my body as I held him close and kissed his soft fur over and over while he licked my cheeks. I loved everything about him—from his soft paws to his sweet breath.

Chris and Dave clamored to hold the puppy too. Reluctantly I handed him to Dave first—'cause my brother wasn't so annoying today.

"Oh, Bob." Mama frowned. "Where did you get

that?" She shook her head slowly.

"A guy at the factory."

Mama's mouth twisted. "You know, puppies are a lot of work."

He reached over and gave her a kiss. "The kids can take care of him." Daddy looked square at me. "Won't you, Alice?" He gave Mama a sideways hug. "You'll see, honey. It'll be fine."

We played with the puppy out in the backyard as Mama finished supper. Full of pep, he bounded around in the grass after us as fast as he could go until he ran out of juice and fell asleep.

Daddy made a bed for him, lining a basket with an old rag rug, and settled him down in the kitchen while we ate supper.

I ate my dumpling, hardly tasting a bite, with one eye on the puppy a few feet away. He was sound asleep, his fat little belly rising and falling with every breath. It was the best day ever.

"Look at that." I said, pointing to the puppy. "He's sucking on that piece of rag."

"He's probably dreaming about being with his mother," Daddy said. "You're going to be his mama now—teach him how to be a good little dog."

"I can be his mama, too," Chris said.

I rolled my eyes. She'd tire of the responsibility by tomorrow.

Mama raised her brows. "After supper when he wakes up, you can give him some milk and a piece of dumpling. It will be your job to watch after him," she said with a stern face. "And that means teaching him not to pee in the house."

"I will, Mama, and I'll take really good care of him," I said. "I promise."

Officially, Mike was our family pet, but neither of my siblings were as excited as I was. I'd been begging for a dog for as long as I could remember. My brother liked animals, but his interest leaned toward critters that creeped most people out—snakes in particular. Chris liked the idea of animals, but interacting with them didn't hold the same appeal.

I knew the puppy was mostly for me, and so it would be my job to care for him. I named him Mike.

Though I didn't know what I was doing, I dedicated myself to his training. Before long he came when I called his name. I lavished him with praise as he learned to sit and stay. I continually took him out to the grass to pee, worried that he'd wet on Mama's rug. Luckily, Mike proved to be an enthusiastic student, and learned the rules before Mama's patience ran out.

I loved that dog with a passion. He was perfect. Affectionate, eager to please, and as bright as any animal ever was.

Mike lived in the house with us. He woke me each morning by licking my face, and we played together endlessly.

He had to be of mixed breed because Daddy would never have paid for a dog when free mongrel pups were always available. But he grew up to look like a border collie. He had all the energy of that breed as well.

No one had fenced-in backyards in our neighborhood, but we had a long clothesline. Daddy devised a sliding leash on the line that allowed Mike to run most of the length of the yard so he could get plenty of exercise.

I confided in Mike all the fears I couldn't share with anyone else. When I was the last to be chosen to play softball at school, he comforted me. When the boys threw snowballs at me on the playground, he cheered me. He patiently listened to my hopes for the future. And, in the ways only a dog can, Mike assured me he loved me and would always be there for me. I promised the same to him.

From sunup to sundown, Mike and I were buddies. When I ate breakfast, so did he. He waited for me when I came from school, elated to see me again. We spent more time playing together in the backyard than most children. He sat at my feet when I did my homework. And when I went to bed at night, Mike was there, assuring me that no monsters lurked in the dark corners.

The summer Mike was three, and I was ten, Daddy bought a black and white television set. They were fairly new then. The miraculous box captivated us kids.

One Tuesday afternoon, we kids were watching television. Daddy was still at work, and Mike was outside on his sliding run. The Gabby Hayes Show had ended, and Howdy Doody had just started. Buffalo Bob asked, "Say kids, what time is it?" Along with the kids in the peanut gallery, we all yelled, "It's Howdy Doody Time!"

That's when I heard squealing brakes out front on the street. We ran outside. A neighbor, Mrs. Kasemeyer, pointed toward our backyard. "I think your dog got hit by a car."

I ran in a panic to the back of the house. My heart raced, and I gasped for breath. Mike lay on his side under our elm tree. He had wriggled out of his collar. After the car struck him, he'd run to our backyard with the last of his strength and collapsed. Blood trickled from his mouth as he whimpered.

An intense pain gripped the back of my throat. In tears, I fell to my knees and reached out to comfort him, but my mother snatched me back and held me.

"He's hurt bad, honey," Mama said. "He may be out of his mind in pain and bite you."

She insisted my brother, sister, and I go with a neighbor, Mrs. Bergmann, to her house to wait until she came to get us.

"No, Mama, please," I begged, my heart breaking. "I gotta stay with Mike. He needs me."

Mama overruled me, and the neighbor I barely knew led us away.

Mrs. Bergmann took us to her kitchen. She gave us cookies and milk, but I couldn't swallow mine. She assured us that God was in control and everything would be as it should be. Inconsolable and afraid, I wasn't so sure she was right. She turned her television on in the living room and set us down in front of it to watch the rest of Howdy Doody, but I didn't hardly see it. My beloved Mike lay in terrible pain under the tree behind our house and I wasn't there to comfort him.

When Mama came to collect us, she said in a

sympathetic tone, "It's all over now. You can come home." We returned to our house, and I ran to where Mike had been lying under the spreading elm. The only thing left of him was a small bloodstain in the grass.

A policeman had been dispatched to put my dying friend out of his misery. I suppose Mama asked him to dispose of Mike's body too.

I collapsed onto the grass where Mike had taken his final breath, and beat the ground with my fists —angry, remorseful, shattered. I sobbed until I was exhausted.

Mama told Daddy about the accident when he came home from work. He put his lips together tight and shook his head. Life went on as normal for everyone else. I was the only one who couldn't eat any supper.

For months afterward, I grieved the loss profoundly. I blamed myself for watching television instead of being with Mike. I dreamed repeatedly that I'd see him alive somewhere. That he wasn't dead at all, that he'd been wandering the streets lost, looking for me.

Mama had tried to shield me from the pain of seeing his body, but there was so much I needed to tell my friend. I'd needed to run my fingers over his fur—to tell him how sorry I was that I left him

alone that afternoon, that I would never forget
what a good dog he was. I needed to tell him I
loved him one last time. Most of all, I needed to
tell my best friend goodbye. But I didn't get to,
and it left a void in my heart that I never quite got
over.

# April, 2019, Saturday, Early Afternoon

Chris's voice jolts me back to the present. "If you're through with your plate, I'll throw it away with mine."

"Yeah, sure, thanks," I say, handing it to her as she rises. I wonder if she sees the tears in my eyes.

Tears don't need to be explained at a memorial event, and I'm glad I don't have to try. How could I tell anyone that the tears were for a dog who's been dead for many decades? That day so many years ago was when I learned the meaning of death, grief, and regret.

Rose approaches and leans down. "Come out to my car." She speaks softly as she touches Chris's knee. "I have something I want to show you both."

I'm happy for the break from the slide show. The presentation is on a loop, and I must have seen all the photos at least four times.

She unlocks and opens the trunk of her car. Rose

unwraps a rifle swaddled in a blanket. I know next to nothing about guns, but it looks like an older model that has been lovingly restored.

"It's beautiful." I finger the smooth stock. "Looks like Dave put in a lot of work on it."

"Yeah, well, you know Dave. He loved guns." She unwraps another one with a telescopic sight, its stock also highly polished. Rose hands it to Chris and unwraps a slightly shorter bundle, holding a shotgun out for me to take.

I'd never handled a shotgun before, and it's heavier than I imagined. I stroke the beautiful walnut gunstock. "Just gorgeous."

She takes out another gun. All of them are in flawless condition. These were clearly treasured items.

Rose caresses the burnished wood of the fourth gun and looks at Chris. "I know you're not likely to want them, but I thought your son might." She pauses. "Guns were Dave's thing, not mine. They should go to someone who will appreciate them—someone in the family."

"Wow," Chris says. "Yeah, I'm sure Darin would love to have one of Dave's guns—but not all four. You should sell the others, Rose. I bet they're valuable. That could help with the funeral expenses."

I nod my agreement and feel a little self-conscious. Chris already sent a sizable check to help pay for the cremation. No one had suggested I do the same, and I hadn't felt like I could. Truth be told, Chris probably sent more than she could afford, but that's my sister. Generous to the core.

"I want Darin to have them." Rose's voice is earnest. "He hunts, doesn't he?"

"Yes, but not that often."

"Well, David didn't actually hunt much—not for quite a while. When we lived in Montana, he did, but it's just been target practice the last few years."

"I wouldn't feel right about taking all four," Chris insists.

"Take two, then." Rose raises her brows. "David would want Darin to have them."

Chris acquiesces, and we carefully re-wrap them, and put them in her car as Rose goes back in the house.

"I've never been hunting in my life or even fired a gun." Chris pushes the guns to the back of the cargo space where they won't be visible. "Have you?"

"No, and I never want to. Nothing about killing animals appeals to me."

She shuts the hatchback. "Me either. I wonder when Dave got so interested in guns. When he and Rose lived in Montana, you think? Or Vietnam?"

"I don't know. I think maybe when he was a kid." We walk back up the driveway to the front door. "Remember when he went rabbit hunting with Daddy and Uncle Alvin? I think he might have been about twelve. The way he carried on afterward, he must have loved it."

"Maybe that's what started it all."

"I'll never forget when they got home"—I pause on the front porch—"Dave came running in the house so excited, dangling a dead rabbit from his hand to show Mama. 'I killed it all by myself.' He didn't even notice the blood dripping onto Mama's clean floor."

"I bet she wasn't so thrilled."

I laugh. "She hollered, 'Get that bloody thing out of my kitchen,' and waved toward the back door." I meet Chris's eyes. "Don't you remember? I'm sure you were there."

"No. Funny how you remember and I don't," Chris says opening the door. "I'm not that much younger than you."

"I guess it's what makes an impression at the time. I was upset that he'd killed a cute cottontail. I couldn't eat the hasenpfeffer Mama made with it. Just didn't seem right. Poor little bunny."

We get something to drink from the kitchen and return to our seats in the living room. All the other guests know each other and are talking among themselves. The slide show goes through its loop again.

"I doubt if Daddy took Dave hunting often," Chris says, "or I'd surely remember it,"

"I don't think he did, and probably only with Uncle Alvin. Fishing was more Daddy's thing."

As if on cue, a slide comes on of Dave holding up a catfish, and then one of him and Daddy together with a stringer of fish. Another photo flashes on the screen, this time it's Dave grasping a frog in each hand, pure delight in his eyes. In the image, there's a tent in the background, and dense woods behind it.

I turn to Chris. "I remember that place. I think I was about ninc."

## Frogs
## Early 1950s


We drove down a narrow country road in central Illinois pulling our 14-foot aluminum boat under a canopy of tree limbs. We hadn't seen farm land or a house for miles.

David yelled, "Look," and pointed to several wild turkeys pecking in the grass beside the road.

Daddy slowed down so we could all get a good look.

"There's nine of 'em," Chris said, bouncing on the seat beside me.

I held my arm out the open window, savoring the warm breeze and the woodsy smell. I loved our vacations, and we had two whole weeks to while away.

Mom held a map in her lap. "I'm not sure we're on the right road. They really ought to post a sign now and then."

"There's one," Daddy said, nodding toward a

wooden sign ahead. He slowed the car to read it: *Grainger Park*. "Let's look around," he said, pulling into one of two parking places. "This might do for a night or two."

As soon as we got out of the car, we heard a gurgling stream. Daddy scrutinized the waterway. "It's deep enough for the boat. I don't think we'll get bogged down."

Mama nodded her approval of the campsite. "I like that there's no one else around. It will be private."

"I gotta go to the bathroom," Chris said.

"We'll have to rough it, honey." Mama motioned for my sister to follow her. "We'll find a nice private place in the woods."

I leaned to look at a bend in the rippling stream. River birch and cottonwoods lined the banks. Blooming aquatic plants along the shoreline lent a magical air to the site. I took a deep breath, filling my lungs with the slightly musty, spicy smell of the slow-moving tributary and the surrounding nature. It was like having our own little piece of paradise.

"Look." David pointed to an egret fishing in the shallows.

"There's an otter," I said as it broke the water's surface before diving into the depths. "Did you see it—did you?"

The stream teemed with life. We saw two more egrets during the first fifteen minutes and a half-dozen different birds.

A splintery picnic table covered with leaves sat in the clearing. It looked as if no one had used it in years. When Mama got back with Chris, she brushed the leaves off the table and cleared the campground of branches and other brush.

David helped Daddy put up our sleeping tents and a tarp over the picnic table. Chris and I gathered dead branches for firewood and piled them up a few feet from the table for Daddy to build a fire later.

When we'd finished, we sat around the table eating lunchmeat sandwiches. The sky was already dusky, and a few bullfrogs were tuning up.

"There must be a million frogs in that creek." Mama took a potato chip from a bag.

"I'll be gigging for those frogs after supper," Daddy said. "We'll eat frog legs for lunch tomorrow." He looked at David. "It's a two-man job, son. Wanna go with me?"

David's eyes brightened. "Yeah. That'll be fun."

He and Daddy got our boat into the water and tied

it to a tree on the bank.

None of us kids had ever been frog-gigging, and we were curious. Daddy fashioned a cane pole with a three-pronged hook suspended from the tip on a foot-long length of fishing line.

"Can I go, too?" I asked Daddy when he had the pole ready.

"Not this time. There isn't room."

"No fair," I said under my breath, sulking.

"Come on, Dave." Daddy grabbed a flashlight and the pole. "Let's go get us some frogs."

Chris and I watched from the bank. The boat glided out over the water, hardly making a sound. I wanted to be in the boat with Daddy and gritted my teeth as I strained to see what they were doing. The trees and rushes at the water's edge obscured our view. Now and then, we saw flashes of their light. In the silence, a cry rang out, "Yes!" David must have caught a frog. Then, it got quiet again.

Not long after, they came back with a half-dozen enormous bullfrogs in a bag. Chris and I clamored for a turn.

"Please, Daddy." I hopped up and down on the shore as David got out of the boat. "I'll do just what you tell me. Can I go now?"

Daddy smiled. "Tie on life preservers real snug, girls. I think we have room for both of you."

"Be real careful." Mom handed the orange jackets to us and cinched them up tight by the light of the waning moon. "We don't want anybody falling in the water when it's so dark."

Chris and I climbed into the boat.

"Bet you don't get as many as I did," David called from the bank.

Daddy handed me the flashlight. "Shine it along the shore as I row."

The boat glided slowly and soundlessly as I swept the light along the water's edge. No one spoke. We listened and searched among the rocks and reeds. A water snake slithered into the rushes, and I glimpsed a big fish just under the surface before I heard a bullfrog croak. I trained the light in that direction and found the frog's unblinking yellow eyes reflected in the beam. Sitting on the bank facing the water, it didn't move—just croaked again.

"It's a big one," my sister said softly. "Let me hold the flashlight." She reached out for it.

"No!" I pushed her hand away. "Daddy told *me* to."

"Shush," Daddy whispered. "Keep the light on him —and I'll show you how it works."

He eased the boat closer until we were a few feet out. I remained perfectly still so I wouldn't rock the boat. Then, as I held the light steady, he dangled the hook until it hung an inch under the frog's chin, then he jerked up.

"Got 'em!" The big bullfrog kicked at the end of the line in the light of the flashlight.

Chris and I whooped softly.

Daddy frowned. "Shush up. You'll scare away the rest." He quickly removed the bullfrog from the barbed gig and dropped it into the bag on the bottom of the boat, then rowed us farther down the shoreline.

"You take a turn now, Alice." He handed me the pole. "I'll get us in position and Chris can hold the light." Daddy sat back, took hold of the oars, and rowed.

He slid the boat along the shoreline as Chris trained the light and we listened. I held my breath when I saw the next frog, and we moved in close. I carefully extended the pole to dangle the hook under its chin. The line touched his nose when I tried to position the barb, and he jumped into the water. My heart sank.

"Can I try again, Daddy?" I whispered. "I know what I did wrong."

Daddy nodded and continued rowing. "Take it slow and easy."

I spotted another big one squatting low beside a moss-covered rock and pointed. Its yellow eyes stared as Daddy eased the boat closer. I held the pole at the ready. When we were a yard or so from the bank, I suspended the hook over him. He croaked in a deep voice as I lowered the three-pronged hook past his glowing eyes and held it as close under his chin as I could without touching him. Then I flicked the gig up and hooked him.

"I got 'em. Got 'em." My heart beat wildly.

Daddy unhooked the frog and added him to the bag. "That was good."

I hooked four more while Daddy rowed and Chris directed the light. Then Chris and I traded seats, and she got to handle the gigging pole while I held the light for her. We hooked nine in all.

When we returned to camp, Daddy killed the frogs quickly, skinned the legs, and put them in a plastic bag in the cooler for Mama to fry the following day. I'd never eaten frog legs before, but Daddy said they tasted like chicken.

David and Mama had a campfire started, and we

sat around it, watching the flames pop and crackle until it burned down to glowing coals. Mama produced a bag of marshmallows, and we toasted them over the embers before turning in. Chris and I shared a small tent and slept on a blow-up air mattress.

That first night, we heard rustling outside, and peeked through the tent flap.

"Raccoons," Chris said. "Two of 'em."

They were at the perimeter of our campsite where Daddy had cleaned the frogs, helping themselves to the discarded remains. We watched them in the moonlight, and most every night after that. The coons were especially fond of the guts Daddy left for them when he cleaned fish. Sometimes, three or four showed up, and when we listened carefully, we could hear their happy chirps and chattering. In the morning, only heads, tails, and bones were left. Daddy took those into the woods and buried them.

My parents had planned to stay only a night or two, but we were having so much fun, they decided we would spend our whole two-week vacation there. Although a gravel road bordered the campground, we saw only two cars go by during the entire time we were there. Every couple of days, Daddy drove ten miles to the nearest town to buy ice and groceries, and we settled into a routine of fishing, frogs, and fun.

We explored along the banks on foot and from the boat. I loved living in nature close to the animals and birds. We spotted lots of turtles sunning themselves on branches sticking out of the water and several kinds of waterbirds, mostly white egrets and ducks.

I walked in the woods close to our camp one morning and spotted a buck munching acorns under an oak tree. I caught my breath. He was beautiful and had antlers just like the pictures on Uncle Alvin's calendar. He didn't see me at first so I stood frozen watching him forage in the leaves. After a minute or two, he noticed me, jumped into the underbrush and disappeared. Mama said she'd seen a doe with a fawn earlier in the week when she was picking a columbine, but just for a split second.

One morning, David came back from a hike excited. "I saw a red fox. It lifted its leg to pee just like a dog. I spotted a snake too. It might have been a king snake, but it got away before I could tell for sure." Later he asked our parents, "If I can catch a snake, can I take it home?"

"No, Dave," Mama said as she pinned a t-shirt on a line Daddy had strung between two trees. "Don't go catching any. I don't want snakes in our camp."

Although Mama cooked all our meals over a campfire, washed our dirty shirts in creek water, and kept the camp organized, she enjoyed our vacations too. Most days she spent some time fishing with a cane pole that had a red-and-white bobber.

Sometimes she went with us on hikes. Mama collected wildflowers and pressed them in a book. She looked them up in her field guide. "This one is an evening primrose," she'd say, or "Look how red this lobelia is" or "Have you ever seen a sweeter little coneflower?" She showed us girls how she spread out the petals and foliage carefully before closing the pages of her book to flatten the blossoms.

"What are you going to do with the wildflowers you press?" I asked.

"I'll put them in a scrapbook with our pictures to remember our vacation."


One afternoon when Chris and I were in the boat with Daddy scouting the creek, I heard a racket and spotted a duck. It flew just over the surface of the stream and dipped down to splash the water, quacking.

"Daddy, what's wrong with that duck?" I pointed. "Is it hurt?"

"No—just trying to get our attention. She has

babies somewhere close, and that's her way of keeping us from noticing them." He smiled at me. "God made her clever, didn't he?"

We scanned the water's edge and finally saw them —several brown-and-yellow little ducklings hiding under overhanging roots. They were so cute and I wanted to get closer, but Daddy said we'd only scare them.

"Their mama will go back to them when we leave. She doesn't know our intentions are friendly." He rowed our boat on down the stream.

Daddy was not a patient fisherman who sat in a boat or on the bank with a line in the water waiting for a fish to bite. He liked to be doing something all the time and wanted the fish to be waiting for him. Trotline fishing was his method. Daddy strung a line with dangling hooks along one area of the bank a few feet from the water's edge. He baited them with stink bait, a nasty-smelling concoction he made at home, and left them overnight. Every morning he checked the hooks along the trotline and usually had at least two catfish on the line.

After dark each night, he took one or two of us kids out to gig for frogs. Mom fried the legs up in a cast-iron skillet over a campfire, and we feasted on fish and frog legs every day for our noon meal, and sometimes for supper too. Chris, though adventurous in other ways, was picky about food, and reluctant to try the frog legs at first. I liked them right off, though they tasted more like fish than chicken.

Every night, we toasted marshmallows over the campfire coals before we went to our tents. The baritone croaks of countless bullfrogs blended with the chirping of cicadas to lull us to sleep.

# April, 2019, Saturday Afternoon

I look at another slide from that vacation. This one shows all three of us holding frogs up for the camera, wide grins on our faces.

Chris leans toward me. "That was a fun vacation, wasn't it? I'd like to go frog gigging again before I die."

"I don't think it would be as much fun now," I say. "I'm not even sure I could enjoy fishing… killing anything."

A fleeting memory surfaces. It was after our visit to Aunt Martha in Iowa, but before the vacation when we learned to gig frogs.

Daddy brought home a half dozen live chickens. I thought he was going to fix nesting boxes for them, and they would lay eggs for us like Aunt Martha's hens.

I found out differently that evening when I ask my dad if they would live in the shed.

"No, Alice," Daddy said. "These chickens are too old to keep—too old to lay eggs."

He'd been raised on a farm and knew about such things; and had done his share of unpleasant chores as a kid.

I watched in horror as my dad chopped off the head of the first chicken. It flapped its wings and ran around the yard spewing blood from its severed neck. The hen's head lay next to the chopping block, its red eye staring up at me.

I ran into the house and threw up my supper.

"Don't let it upset you," Mama told me. "That's what chickens are for. They lay eggs for three or four years, and then they go in a stew pot." It hadn't occurred to me during the visit to the farm that many of the animals were destined for a dinner plate.

I couldn't eat the chicken and dumplings Mama made the next day. I kept thinking about Mimi, the docile hen I'd befriended on the farm, and the sweet sound she made when I petted her. Did she end up in a stew on Aunt Martha's table? It wasn't fair. Wasn't it enough that we took their eggs away?

Was it so different from watching my father kill

the fish and frogs on vacation? I couldn't reconcile the memories.

I try to get back into that mindset—to understand the paradox, but I can't come up with an adequate rationale. Perhaps it was that from my earliest memories I'd watched Daddy clean fish and Mama fry them, and I accepted those creatures that lived in the water as not quite animals, but food. Whatever the reason, there is no denying that I loved it.

That silly grin on my face in the picture stays in my mind as another slide comes on. I loved animals, yet there I was—giddy after killing one.

I glance at the clock in Rose's brother's living room as the slide show begins another cycle. Other than Chris, I've barely spoken to anyone at the open house. She's chatted with a few others, but Rose's family are mostly catching up with each other's lives.

I lean toward my sister. "I'm feeling invisible. I wish someone from our side of the family would show up soon. We've been sitting here over an hour." I sigh. "I hadn't planned to spend the whole afternoon here."

"Me neither, but we can't very well leave until

they get here. It's a come-and-go affair, so they're not really late."

I fidget in my chair and push my sleeves up and down, listening for their arrival.

This is the fifth memorial for family members in my generation. We buried Mama eleven years ago —the last of her sisters to die, but we have cousins around. Steve and his daughter are driving up from Tulsa, as well as Kathy and her husband from Bartlesville. Janet promised to come with her sister and their husbands. She's the only one who lives nearby and knew Dave as an adult, although she's twenty years younger, and the only cousin I communicate with regularly.

I sit back and try to relax while watching the now familiar series of slides on the big screen.

My mind wanders as pictures trigger memories, taking me back to the secluded campground, next to the gurgling stream.

## Gypsies
## Early 1950s


"Mama, can Chris and I go out fishing in the rowboat?" I asked one afternoon. We'd been camping for five days and Daddy had been teaching us to row.

She looked up from peeling potatoes for supper. "If your father says you can."

I scurried off and found Daddy collecting firewood in the woods.

"Daddy, Mama says if it's okay with you, Chris and I can take the rowboat out fishing."

He cocked his head thoughtfully. "Okay. Wear the jackets and don't go too far. I want to hear you if you call."

I grinned and ran back to camp to tell Chris. We gathered our fishing poles, donned the life preservers and slid the boat out onto the water. Sitting side-by-side, we both rowed, looking for a wide place in the stream to try our luck.

We'd just baited our hooks near a grassy bend and plopped them in the creek when we noticed the water roiling in a small inlet closer to the bank.

"What's going on over there?" Chris asked.

I was curious too. "Let's get closer and see."

We pulled our lines out of the water, and each of us handling an oar, rowed closer. An enormous fishtail and then the whole side of a fish broke the water's surface.

"Those are monster fish," Chris said. "Why are they rolling around in the water like that?"

We slid our boat into the middle of the activity. The water seemed shallow, and I hoped we wouldn't get stuck. The fish didn't pay any attention to us as they churned the water beside us.

The dip net Daddy used to scoop up big fish when he ran his trotlines rested on the bottom of the boat. "I bet if we held the net over the side, we could catch one of those fish."

Chris grabbed the net, and we both took hold of the long handle and stuck it down in the middle of the writhing mass. Water splashed and the net almost jerked out of our hands. We had netted something but couldn't see very well. It took both of us pulling as hard as we could to lift the thrashing net out of the water and into the boat.

"Wow, I can't believe it," Chris said. Two huge fish flailed about in the net

"They're gigantic," I said. "Mama and Daddy will be so surprised. Let's go show them!"

We pushed our oars against the bottom of the creek to get us out of the inlet. Hearts pounding and faces flush with excitement, we headed back as fast as we could to our camp as the fish flopped in the boat's bottom.

"Mama! Daddy! Look what we caught!" Chris hollered when we neared our campsite.

I couldn't get the words out fast enough as Daddy strode toward us to help with the boat. "We caught giant fish! Two of them. In the net. Come see 'em Daddy."

"We just put the net in the water and they jumped in," Chris said, the boat rocking as we hurried to get out.

Daddy tied the boat to a tree at the water's edge. "I don't think it's legal to catch fish that way." He shook his head when he saw them. "Carp. They were probably spawning."

I thought I saw a smile cross his lips, but then he frowned. "Never do that again!"

"Oh," I hung my head and felt hot all over.

"Okay," I said in unison with my sister. I didn't know what spawning meant, but we must have done something bad. Daddy didn't really act like he was mad, but I thought he'd be proud of us.

"If it's wrong, maybe we could put them back?" I said.

Daddy shook his head. "No, it's too late for these fish. See their eyes are glassy and they aren't flopping anymore."

"I felt sad for the fish, and a lead lump of guilt sat in my stomach because we had broken the law." Daddy and Mama taught us to do what was right.

"But wasting them would be more wrong," he explained, and took the big fish to clean.

Mama fried the carp for supper, but none of us liked them as much as catfish and frog legs. Too many bones. Picking them out was more work than it was worth. We placed the leftovers out at the perimeter of the camp for the raccoons. In the morning they were gone.

After we'd been camping there for a little more than a week, a car pulled off the road while Daddy was cleaning fish. Big letters spelled Sheriff on the side of the vehicle.

When I saw the uniformed officer's frown as he walked toward Daddy, I was sure he'd heard what

Chris and I had done. I looked at my sister. Her mouth was wide open and her eyes round.

"We've had a complaint that gypsies are living in the park," the sheriff said. "I guess they meant you folks."

"We're not living here," Daddy said, as Mama joined him.

The sheriff glanced around at the three tents; the clothes drying on the line strung between trees, Daddy's fish cleaning bench, and the folding chairs around the gray coals of last night's fire. "Sure looks to me like somebody is."

Mama put her hands on her hips. "We are not living here and we are not gypsies. We live in a proper house over in Quincy."

Daddy explained. "We're just here for a few days —on vacation."

"Camping isn't allowed in this park," the officer said. "Just picnicking and hiking. Fishing, stuff like that."

"There's no signs." Still clutching the bloody knife he'd used to cut the head off a catfish, Daddy motioned with his hand around the campsite. "We're way out in the woods."

The officer stepped back with his hand on his belt.

"Put the knife down, sir."

Daddy complied. "What I mean is, we're not bothering anybody way out here, and it doesn't look like anyone has even picnicked here for ages. What's the harm?"

"The law's the law." The officer took a deep breath. "Might be best if you folks moved along. People can get pretty riled up. We had a band of gypsies through these parts last summer, and there were some issues. I think it would be better for everyone if you took your family and left the county tomorrow morning."

When the sheriff drove away, Chris asked, "What are gypsies, Mama?"

"They don't live in houses, and they travel around, and some of them don't obey the law."

We broke camp the next morning, three days early, and left our little piece of paradise. As we pulled out, Chris asked, "Are we gypsies, Mama?"

"You girls might be." Daddy chuckled. "I hear gypsies are real good at catching carp."

## April, 2019, Saturday, Afternoon

The doorbell rings, and our cousins arrive en masse. We exchange hugs with all eight of them. Rose's family greets them warmly and invites them to have some refreshments, but it is obvious they are just dropping by. They don't even sit. We visit for maybe fifteen minutes, and they say they need to get going. They are trying to fit in visits to several friends during the weekend. Janet is using a walker and tells us she needs to rest.

"We're meeting at six at Sprouts Restaurant. You'll come, won't you?" My cousin, Steve, asks me as they say their goodbyes. "We can catch up more then."

"We'll be there," Chris says.

I wish they had stayed a while, but I understand. David never had much to do with our extended family after he was grown. Much older than any of the cousins, he hadn't hung around with them even as a kid. He was only two years older than me, but after he left home, I hardly saw him, myself. It seems clear: our cousins have gathered in Quincy mostly to see one another, and the memorial was just the catalyst for the reunion.

A few minutes after they go, Chris and I leave too.

"It's been good to see you, Rose," I say, embracing her at the door. "Let us know how you're doing. We need to keep in touch." Even as I say it, I doubt if we will. The morning Rose called with news of Dave's death was the only time she'd ever phoned. And my efforts to maintain a connection, even when Dave was alive, were dismal.

"Thanks again for the guns for Darin," Chris says, laying a light hand on Rose's arm. "I know they will mean a lot to him."

As we drive away, Chris meets my eyes for a moment. "We've got over three hours before dinner. I don't want to spend it at the hotel. What do you want to do?"

"I need a cup of coffee. I thought they'd have some with the refreshments."

A few minutes later, Chris sits across the table from me at a McDonald's and sips a hot chocolate. "Was the open house what you expected?"

"I guess. I knew it would be a little awkward since I don't know Rose's family."

"Maybe it's just my imagination," Chris says, "but

I kind of got the impression David didn't fit into that family any more than he did in ours after he came home from Vietnam—even before that, really. There sure weren't any pictures of him with her family. Lots of him and Rose, but not one with her family except their wedding picture."

"You know when you think about it, a lot of our old family pictures are of you and me together and then photos of Dave by himself." I sigh. "But then what boy wants to hang around his little sisters?"

"He did mostly keep to himself."

"I wonder how happy he was." I take a sip of coffee. "We talked when we were teenagers—really talked—but it's been years since we had a heart-to-heart. It's my fault as much as his. We had so little in common."

"I think he was happy." Chris wipes at a drop of cocoa on the table with a napkin and adjusts the lid on her cup. "We didn't talk that much either, and when we did, it was mostly superficial stuff—what they'd been doing."

"You made more of an effort than I did." I look down at my cup and take a pained breath. "Maybe if I had tried harder to keep the lines of communication open, I wouldn't feel so crappy now."

Neither of us spoke for a while. I thought of an incident when we were in our twenties and my husband, Warren, along with our kids, were in Quincy for a visit. I'd been outspoken to Dave about how he was complicating Mom and Daddy's life. He'd gotten into drugs while he was in the service, split up with his first wife, and quit his job. He seemed content to mooch off our parents. That blunt exchange had colored our interactions ever since.

"After he came home from the navy, I was rough on him for not taking responsibility for his own life," I say. "I'm sure I came off as self-righteous. I knew I was right and he was wrong." I pause and sigh. "I should have cut him a little slack. I think he was doing the best he could then."

Chris shook her head. "It's easy to look back and second guess ourselves. When we're in our twenties, we think we have it all figured out. But we were doing the best we could at the time too."

"I think after Dave left home, he wasn't that close with anyone in the family, least of all Daddy," I say. "His time in the navy changed him, and his marriage to Karen. That was a disaster all the way around."

"It couldn't have started off worse—with her telling him she was pregnant when she wasn't. He tried to do the right thing, and it all backfired."

"That's no way to start a marriage," I say, "but at the time I wasn't too sympathetic. I don't look at things so black and white now." I inhale deeply. "The divorce sure didn't help his relationship with Mama and Daddy either."

"I wish Daddy would have been on the same wavelength with David when he was growing up," Chris says. "I always felt like he wasn't the kind of dad David needed. You know?"

"They both liked to talk… and they both liked the outdoors," I say. "That was something."

"Yeah, but that was about it. David was always reading, and not that interested in working on cars, machinery—the things Daddy liked." She looks at me. "They never really clicked. I think Daddy just didn't know what to do with a boy like Dave."

"I think he tried when Dave was a kid, but you're probably right, especially when he got to be a teenager. I think the only interaction they had then was at the dinner table—and there was no real connection there. It just highlighted their differences."

"Did you know that's one reason I hung out down at the shed with Daddy so much? I thought I could make up for David not being into any of that stuff."

"I didn't know that." I tilt my head trying to remember. "I guess that was why you weren't up with me in the kitchen helping Mama with supper."

"Yep." She chuckles. "I was with Daddy trying to be the son he didn't have, watching him overhaul an engine or repair something or other."

I take a sip of my coffee and smile at my sister. "You always were nicer than me."

Chris grins and doesn't contradict me. She knows it's true. I never quite got the hang of being diplomatic. I don't talk much, but when I do, I'm apt to be too pointed.

"It's a wonder we get along as well as we do," I say. "It's not like we are that much alike. It amazes me some of the extraordinary lengths you go to accommodate others. Me—I find it easy to tell people no."

"Yeah, and people still like you. That's what amazes me."

I feign offense. "At least they always know where they stand with me."

"I bet we could make a long list of how different we are if we tried," Chris says.

"And you'd probably alphabetize the list." I laugh.

"I mean you even alphabetize your spice cabinet."

"I always know where things are." Chris lifts her chin. "Any job worth doing is worth doing well. Your motto is 'good enough.'"

"Only when it's true. I can be meticulous if the job demands it, but why waste time on unimportant things?"

"That's what my boss always said. I'd tell him, 'I don't do quick and dirty.' He learned not to give me a job if he didn't want it done right."

"Yep—that's my sister. No matter how long it takes." I shake my head and smile.

"And yet, you and I never argue—not since we grew up, anyway. Astonishing, isn't it?" Chris says. "You know, friends tell me all the time that they wish they had the kind of relationship with their sister that we have."

"I hear that, too. You'd think people would outgrow sibling rivalry when they become adults." I drink the last of my coffee and scoot my chair out. "I was talking about that the other day with Warren and he said, 'Chris could get along with anybody.' If both of us were like me, he thinks we'd be butting heads all the time."

Chris chuckles. "You are a little bossy."

"I guess I am. But you invite it. You are so easily led." I give her a silly grin.

"That must be the secret," Chris says stuffing her napkin in her empty cup and standing. "I got lots of practice following Michael when he was alive. I loved the man, but it always had to be his way."

"He was fortunate to have you. Any other woman would have declared war when he made unilateral decisions that affected you."

Chris grimaces. "True." We walk toward the door. "I'm glad Dave and Rose got along so well."

"Yeah. She was good for him. They seemed like two peas in a pod. Who else would put up with his menagerie?" I open the door for Chris. "Did she say she found a home for that huge boa constrictor?"

"Yeah, she did. I wonder if she'll keep the parrot and both mastiffs."

"If she does, she won't ever have to worry about intruders."

Chris opens the driver's side door and hesitates before getting in. "We didn't decide where to go next. What do you want to see now?"

"We could drive by Berrian School. We haven't done that yet." I duck in her car and buckle up.

"Berrian it is." Chris pulls out of the McDonald's parking lot and heads south again to the old German part of town. We pass our house on Adams Street and on to our old elementary school, driving the three-block route we walked when we were children.

The neighborhood looks much like it did when we were kids, but a tall chain-link fence surrounds the school yard.

She parks and we get out of the car and walk over to the wire barrier. "It's kind of sad that school playgrounds have to be fortified now like prison yards," I say. "I liked it better in the old days."

"You mean back in the Stone Age." Chris chuckles.

"Yeah, it almost seems that way now. Attitudes have changed so much since we went here."

"It was a simpler time—more gentle."

"I don't much like what the world is becoming," I say. "It's not just more complicated. Decency seems almost quaint now."

Chris nods "I'm glad I'm not young anymore."

"Me too." I take a deep breath and try to shake off the mood as I peer up at the rectangular Georgian-style structure. Emblazoned over the triple arches of the entrance reads Berrian School 1904 in gold relief. The school is not as impressive as many of Quincy's historic architectural treasures, but when we attended, it seemed imposing. This century-old building is an integral part of the tapestry of our childhoods.

We stand quietly looking through the metal links for a while. I position my phone over a hole to take a photo. "The building looks the same—maybe smaller—but everything else is so different." I make a sweeping gesture across the rubber-surfaced school yard with its colorful plastic playground equipment. "A row of viburnum grew along there where the fence is now. We called them snowball bushes, remember?" I sigh. "It softened the look—made the place look friendlier. Not that I was that crazy about school back then."

Chris catches my eye and frowns. "You didn't like Berrian?"

"I just never felt like I fit in—mostly kept to myself. Not like you; in grade school you had lots of friends."

"Did other kids not talk to you?"

"Not that so much as the other way around. I don't

think I knew how to make friends back then. I didn't talk unless I had something significant to say, and I rarely did."

"Yeah, you're still more or less quiet, I guess." Chris glances at me. "Me, I liked school then." She gazes out over the playground with a wistful expression. "I wonder if they still play the same games we did. Do you remember hopscotch and jumping rope? Norma Myers and I got pretty good at double dutch."

"I remember the other kids playing them, but I liked the swings. I didn't think about it then but maybe because that was something I could do alone. I didn't really have any school friends until junior high. I endured grade school." I shake my head slowly as a lump emerges in my throat. "Especially third grade with Mrs. Cravens."

I'm suddenly nine years old again, sitting in the back of the classroom, waiting my turn to stand up front and give my report.

## Book Report
## Early 1950s

My turn was coming. There was no escape. One by one, my classmates stood in front of the room to read their book reports aloud. The dread in my gut deepened as each student finished and sat back down. My palms were sweaty; I worried I might throw up. Some of the kids seemed to enjoy it. A few seemed nervous, but not one of them looked scared.

I had read the book, and written my report, but the thought of standing up there with everyone's eyes on me struck such terror in me, I couldn't stop shaking. I would have given anything to get out of it. I prayed for a fire drill, for an urgent message from Principle Maxwell that required our teacher to leave, for Tommy McGrady to start a fight and have to be disciplined—anything that might delay my doom.

My stomach hurt when I woke up that morning. "Mama, I don't feel so good," I complained.

Mama knew about the report and put a palm to my

forehead. "No fever."

"But Mama, I feel really sick. I just can't go today."

"Sorry, honey, but you have to."

She'd handed me my lunch bag and with a pat on my back, shuffled me out the door with my sister and brother. I would have to face my fate before the jury in Mrs. Craven's courtroom.

Marshall Dunne stepped to the front to read his report. I would go next. I don't know if he did well or not. Marshall's voice echoed from a place far away. My heart pounded in my ears drowning out everything else.

I could hardly catch my breath when he finished and walked back to his desk.

"Alice, it's your turn." The words sucked all the air out of the room, and the floor shifted under me when I rose on wobbly legs and staggered toward my death.

From the front of the classroom, I peered at Mrs. Craven sitting at her desk, but saw no pity in her eyes, no last-minute reprieve.

I faced my judges and then stared at the paper in my hand. My mouth was dry, and I was in danger of wetting my pants. I took a deep breath, and then another and another. They didn't help. Sweat trickled down my neck, and I became dizzy.

"Go on, Alice. Read your report. We're listening." The teacher's voice sounded like she was underwater. "Or just tell us about the book if you'd rather."

I'm not sure if I read anything or spoke at all. If I did, I didn't hear myself. I could hear nothing but a rumble in my head like a freight train roaring down the tracks.

The next thing I knew I was waking up. I thought I was in my bed until I opened my eyes. Above me, the fluorescent light bars flickered, and the floor was hard and cold. A chill shot through me.

I groaned and Mrs. Craven's face hovered over me. She touched my cheek. "Alice? Alice, dear, are you okay?"

Behind her, several of my classmates stared, their eyes wide. I was confused and my cheeks burned with embarrassment. I wanted to sink into the floor and disappear forever.

## April, 2019, Saturday Afternoon

"At least after fainting dead away in her class," I say. "She never made me stand in front of the room again."

"Was that the first time you fainted?" Chris asks.

"The first time was when I was standing on a chair for Mama to braid my hair. I was getting tired—light headed—but Mama told me to hold still until she finished. Then I just keeled over." I chuckle. "After fainting several times when I was young, I finally learned that just because an adult told me to stand there, didn't mean I had to do it until I passed out."

"That was probably why Mama always said you were 'frail' and Daddy called you a 'hot-house plant'."

I roll my eyes. "I'll live to be a hundred."

A rain drop hits my forehead. The sky had been clear all day, but now gray clouds have built to the west of us, and it sprinkles in earnest.

"Oh, no," Chris says, sprinting to the car. "I don't want to get my hair wet. I'll never get it in shape for dinner tonight."

"If you had a short no-fuss cut like I do, you'd never have to worry."

"Maybe when I'm old," Chris says, laughing, as she slides behind the wheel.

She doesn't start the car right away. We sit watching the rain as it pours. Thunder crashes close by and I startle. "Wow, that was a good one." I always did love a good thunderstorm.

## Thunderstorm
## Early 1950s

Thunder boomed. I blinked awake to a lightning flash followed by another boom. I opened the window over my bed. If Mama knew, she'd be mad and scold me. I sat on my knees with my arms folded on the sill and surveyed the sky. In the twin bed a few feet from mine, Chris turned over and pulled the covers over her head.

I waited for another jagged streak of fire to light up the darkness and rumble through the window frame. The white curtain fluttered as a moisture-laden wind blew through the screen to brush across my cheeks and tickle my bare shoulders. I took a deep breath, savoring the sweet scent of rain, eager for the storm to arrive. Like waiting for a present on Christmas morning, I hoped an honest-to-goodness thunder storm would roar through and toss rain and leaves every which way. Storms made me feel more alive, though I didn't have the words for it. I only knew I loved them.

A brilliant lightning bolt lit up the midnight sky outside my bedroom window. Much closer this time, a piercing crack followed a split second later. I jumped. My sister turned over in bed, her head still covered.

An owl sitting on the clothesline post in the glow of the backdoor light spread its great wings and took flight, disappearing into the darkness.

The rain began with big wet polka dots on the cement path that led down to the shed. They got closer together until the walkway was completely wet. The drops were so heavy, water splashed back up as it hit the concrete. A refreshing spray blew through my window, spattering my face and the sill. The elm tree behind the house became shrouded by a gray curtain of rain and looked almost like a ghost. Now and then, a spectacular bolt blazed across the black canopy, bathing the backyard with an eerie radiance. The thunder rumbled for several moments.

The raging storm moved on after a little while. I closed my window and curled up under my covers again, inexplicably comforted.

I wondered if Daddy had been awake and watching the storm. He liked them too—the louder, the better.

When he was home from work and we were still up, he'd let us kids sit with him in the screened-in back porch and watch the world have a hissy fit.

The cool, damp wind whipped through the screens. It was almost like being outside.

The best storms came with hail, but that didn't happen often. The last time was two years ago when I was ten.

That hail storm had been so much fun. My skin had tingled with excitement when ice chunks pounded on our tin roof. It was so loud; I put my hands over my ears and giggled.

After the worst of the deluge, I spotted a big hailstone in the backyard. "Daddy, can I get that one to keep in the freezer?"

"Shh." He put his finger to his lips. "Just one and hurry back," he whispered.

I ran out into the waning storm and grabbed the frozen treasure, bigger than a golf ball but jagged and milky. I raced back to the porch, laughing. "Look, Daddy. It's huge!"

My mother didn't like storms and had stayed in the kitchen. "Bob," she called out to the porch. "Keep that child inside. She could get killed."

Daddy glanced at me and winked. He'd inspected the big chunk of ice, admired its size and shape, and reverently placed it in the freezer.

## April, 2019, Saturday Afternoon

Chris and I sit in the car while the rain beats down around us. "I still love thunder and lightening," I say. "Maybe as much as Daddy did."

"Even now, I can picture that look Daddy got in his eyes when he watched a good thunderstorm?" Chris smiles. "I think it was awe he was feeling."

"I remember that look." I say. "I know exactly how he felt. It's awesome to witness all that power."

"Makes all us people seem small, feeble. Know what I mean? We're not in charge."

I nod. "Exactly. And that's kind of reassuring."

"Especially now… when you think about what's happening in our society—in the world."

A gust of wind slams rain against the passenger side window. I startle. "I wouldn't like to be on the wrong side of all that power."

We sit in silence as I look at the Berrian building, obscured now by a veil of water. It feels oddly appropriate that it should be in a haze the last time I see it. Berrian is part of the past, and I wouldn't want to bring it back.

"Looks like the storm is about over." I glance at the display on my phone. We still have some time before we need to dress for dinner. "Wanna drive by the old church building before we go back to the hotel? If it's still raining we don't have to get out, but it would be nice to see it again. We spent a lot of time there."

"The junior high is on the way; we might as well swing by there again too." Chris starts the car and we pull away from our old elementary school, saddened by the changes it represents.

By the time we've driven the mile to the junior high building, the rain has stopped and Chris turns off the wipers. She drives slowly past the imposing structure, with its Gothic arches, pillars, and gargoyles. The leaded glass windows sparkle after the rain.

"I wish we could go inside now that they've finished the restoration." The last time we were in Quincy, the renovation was underway, and a contractor even took us on a tour. I look up at one of the ornate brick and stone pillars with tall, cathedral-style windows. "I'm sure it's all locked up now."

Chris glances at me. "I bet it's gorgeous."

I sit quietly for a moment and let out a long sigh. "Just think, all that splendor was lost on us when we went to school here. We were so caught up in our own little worlds. What mattered were our classes, our friends."

"Friends?" Chris clears her throat. "Maybe for you, but I didn't have nearly as many friends at junior high—or high school either."

I search my memory. "I guess I didn't think much about it then. I do remember you being more reserved after grade school. Grandma Ivy's nickname for you didn't fit anymore."

"Pistol, you mean?"

"Right," I say. "You weren't as gregarious. I never questioned why you changed. Never wondered about it in all these years. But it was almost like we switched places—in that respect, anyway. Not quite, I guess, I was still not outgoing, but I finally had a good friend."

Chris stares into the distance, then turns away and frowns. "I've never figured out why, but when I went to junior high, the friends I had at Berrian chummed around with other kids. I'd expected it to stay the same, that we'd still be buddies. I was devastated, and I guess I withdrew. I began to think there was something wrong with me."

I felt a stab of guilt. I hadn't really known what was going on in her head back then. I remember being annoyed when we were teenagers because Chris always wanted to do what my friend, Kathy, and I were doing. I think I might even have told her to get her own life and quit trying to piggyback on mine.

"Your personality did change—at least temporarily." I smile. "You know, before you came down to college, I told Warren you were shy. Then when you showed up, you were like a different person—a lot like you were as a kid." I chuckle. "Warren said, 'Chris isn't anything like you said she was.'"

"You know why, don't you?" She glances at me. "No one knew me in Oklahoma except you. I was tired of feeling so uptight I couldn't be myself, and I decided to just… just…"

"Let it all hang out?" We both laugh. "I'm glad you did. It was nice to have my fun-loving sister back."

On a whim, we swing by the high school.

"This is a different building." I scrunch up my nose as Chris slows the car. "The one we attended was in that 50s space-age style that never looked quite permanent—and it was fairly new."

"Evidently it *wasn't* permanent." Chris chuckles. "It's been well over fifty-five years ago, though. We can't expect everything to stay the same."

"Let's go on. I've got good memories from high school, but they weren't in that building."

We drive a few blocks farther and park outside the old church.

A warm wave washes over me as I survey the church building. Nothing has changed except for the name on the sign out front. The congregation now meets elsewhere, but this is where our memories reside.

Chris turns off the engine. "I think our lives were shaped here as much as at home, and definitely more than at any school. Our youth group wasn't so cliquey as the kids at school."

"We were lucky to have such a great youth group at church, especially during those crazy, early teen years." I lean back against the headrest and think about the kids in our group. I still keep track of several of them on Facebook. In my mind they are all young like they were when we spent so much time together. "I really loved our picnics, parties, and youth rallies—even the work days…"

Chris holds up a finger. "And summer camp."

"Yeah. I loved camp. You did too, right?"

"Except for having to shower in front of the other girls. Camp was different from school. It felt friendlier, and we got to know the other kids right away. I didn't feel like an outsider there."

"You know, I kissed a boy for the first time at church camp."

"You never told me that!" Chris's face brightens.

## Camp LaMoine
## Mid-1950s


Sixty campers—seventh and eighth graders—
gathered at long tables to eat our evening meal
with a half-dozen counselors. Hot dogs never had
much appeal for me but at camp they weren't so
bad.

Sharon Langton, sitting beside me on the wooden
bench, shooed a fly away from her pork and beans.
"That boy keeps looking at you," she whispered,
nodding toward the end of our table.

Sharon was from Macomb, a small town fifty
miles north. Her bunk was next to mine, and we
became friends the first day we met after
discovering we both liked the outdoors, drawing,
and best of all, animals.

"What boy?" I glanced in the direction she
indicated.

"The one with the reddish hair. Do you know
him?"

"Not really." I smothered my hot dog with more

ketchup. "He's on my team. Dwight, I think his name is." I stole another look at him and frowned. "What's he looking at me for?"

Sharon giggled. "I think he likes you."

If I'd had a type at the tender age of thirteen, Dwight wouldn't have been it. Gangly with an overbite more prominent than his chin, he had a mop of orange hair badly in need of a trim.

Not that I was particularly appealing. Still flat-chested, I dressed plainly and tried to be invisible. Lace was for the pretty girls who had something to show off. My straight black hair, cropped short, suited my no-frills persona.

I looked forward to summer church camp every year since the first one when I was nine. I got to spend all day with other kids my age—no parents, no homework, no chores, and fun activities.

The counselors divided us into four teams of fifteen kids. We competed in contests, played games, shared meals, and put on skits. Mostly we just had fun. I always made a new best friend for the duration. Camp was way more fun than playing with my brother and sister.

But it was more than that. I loved the woodsy smell of being outdoors, meeting around the flagpole every morning at first light as our counselors raised Old Glory. I enjoyed singing with other campers, just being together—and the quiet times, too, when we were free to explore the nature trails, read, or just think.

In the cool of the evening, all the campers gathered together quietly at the vesper service for a time of reflection and prayer as the sun sank in the western sky.

The day always ended with singing around a campfire in the middle of a clearing in the woods. As sparks and smoke drifted into the dark sky, it felt like I was a part of something wonderful.

I ate the last bite of my hot dog, and Sharon whispered to me again. "I bet Dwight wants to be your boyfriend."

"No," I said. It was inconceivable.

Before she could say anything else, one boy stood up and started to sing.

*"Be kind to your web-footed friends."*

We all joined in singing the silly song at the top of our lungs.

*"For a duck may be somebody's mother.*
*Be kind to your friends in the swamp.*
*Where the weather is very, very damp.*
*Now you may think this is the end.*

*Well, it is!"*

We laughed and stood to leave the dining hall. Sharon was heading out to practice with her team for the talent competition when Dwight approached me.

"Hey… Alice?" His voice was low, almost apologetic, and his cheeks flushed red. "Wanna walk with me to campfire tonight?" That was the equivalent of dating at camp.

I froze, stunned into silence. I'd never had a boyfriend and never gone on a date. I sort of liked a boy in my Sunday school class back home. Kenny Schmitt was a year older, but he'd shown no interest in me. No one had until Dwight.

I opened my mouth. All that came out was "Uh." My thoughts were in a jumble. It never occurred to me to say *no*, even to a gawky, freckled-faced adolescent I had no interest in. My hand shook as I picked at a spot on my shirt. "Yeah, I guess."

I don't know why I agreed. He was nice enough, smart, but gawky. Perhaps I didn't want to hurt his feelings. It did feel nice to be asked.

"I'll meet you after vespers." He pointed to a cottonwood tree near the open-air shelter where they held the evening service. "Over there?"

I swallowed hard, looked at the tree and mumbled.

"Ah… Yeah, okay."

In our free time after supper, I went to the girls' tent and lay on my cot. A center aisle ran down the middle of the enormous space with army-surplus cots lined up on either side. Orange crates separated the cots. They held our clothes and everything else we brought along.

To keep from thinking about my date, I tried to memorize a Bible verse or two so my team could earn points toward winning the trophy and chocolates awarded at the end of the week. I read the verses over and over, but couldn't concentrate. All I could think about was Dwight. I chewed on my fingernails until the call came for vespers.

"Dwight asked me to walk with him to campfire tonight," I told Sharon when we met to attend the service.

"I told you he liked you." She grinned. "Are you going to?"

I shrugged. "I guess."

"He seems nice." She grinned.

I felt my face heat up.

I sat with Sharon during vespers the way I had every night. Dwight sat three rows ahead of us and looked back at me every so often.

When the service ended, it was dark, and the kids were gathering to walk to the campfire. A knot grew in the pit of my stomach. I stood under the cottonwood tree, not knowing which frightened me most: that Dwight would show up or that he wouldn't. I didn't know what to do or how I was supposed to feel.

Dwight found me and without a word held out his hand. He smiled like Howdy Doody, the goofy puppet from the television show. I couldn't back out. Other kids held hands as they walked to campfire, so I took his hand. It was sweaty, and I felt awkward as we proceeded toward the clearing in the woods.

Everyone gathered around the campfire and sat on logs, and we sang as the flames popped and crackled. He loosened his grip, and I let go, relieved to have my hand back.

I didn't look at him—just stared into the fire as the smoke rose to the treetops. I wondered what happened after you walked with a boy to campfire. I had only a vague idea of what was expected, but I wasn't going to act like an ignorant kid who knew nothing about boy-girl relationships. I pretended I was experienced and it was all normal.

Dwight took my hand again to walk back to the campground. We didn't talk. I spotted Sharon with a group of girls. She waved, raising her brows with a question in her eyes. I grimaced, torn between wanting to go with Sharon and acting like a pretty girl who had a boyfriend. But Dwight held tight to my hand, so I went along.

He pointed with his free hand to a park bench under a spreading mulberry tree over by the dining hall. "Wanna sit and talk?"

"I guess so." I followed Dwight's lead. This was all uncharted territory.

With a bright moon above us, I perched on the edge the bench beside Dwight. My hands trembled and my belly roiled, unsure of what to say or how to act.

He rested his arm on the back of the bench behind me. "Can I kiss you?"

I didn't want to kiss Howdy Doody—didn't want to be there at all, but I'd come this far. I puckered up and faced him.

I should have shut my eyes. His nose and lips grew bigger and bigger as they got closer.

His mouth was wet and mushy on mine. It was disgusting, but there was no way I was going to show it. I wasn't a kid anymore. Kisses were supposed to be romantic. I'd seen movies. I was determined to play the part I had seen on the screen. I sighed and looked at the moon and hoped

I was convincing. But more than that, I hoped no one had seen us in the shadow of the mulberry tree.

"The fire was… big… I mean tonight… specially," he said.

"Yeah, big, and hot." I tried again. "I mean it seemed hotter."

"Cause it was bigger," he offered, then changed the subject. "Our team. We got a chance, you think? The talent competition?"

"Don't know. You?"

"No, not really."

Neither of us seemed capable of putting together a coherent sentence. After several uncomfortable minutes, we said good night.

So relieved it was over, I wiped my lips on my sleeve to erase the kiss as I hurried to the girls' tent.

The sides of the tents were rolled down for privacy. Sharon was getting ready for bed when I came in.

"Tell me all about it," she said, her brown eyes wide with curiosity. "You didn't look like you were having much fun when I saw you."

"I wasn't, but he wanted to sit and talk for a while." I didn't want to tell her we kissed.

"So?"

"So, nothing," I said, holding up my hand. "We talked."

She didn't press.

Under the covers on my cot with the smell of smoke still lingering in my hair, I wondered if the kiss made him my boyfriend, and what to expect the next day.

I turned over, facing Sharon. "What do you think I should do if Dwight invites me to walk with him to campfire again? I don't want to be his girlfriend."

"He probably knows that already. You weren't exactly beaming."

I turned over and thought about Sharon's comment. She was right. I'd felt miserable the whole time we were together. I couldn't sleep for a long time, but when I woke up, I realized it was just a stupid kiss. I didn't have to be Dwight's girlfriend if I didn't want to.

I avoided him the next day. For the rest of the week, I sat as far away from him as possible at our team meetings, never meeting his eyes. He didn't talk to me again, either. Maybe the kiss wasn't what he expected, and he didn't want to repeat it any more than I did.

It would be four more years before I kissed another boy. That kiss was dreamy, not at all like kissing Howdy Doody.

## April, 2019, Saturday Afternoon

Three purple martins fly between the old church building and our car. "I remember those birds from when we started going to church." I smile at Chris. "Instead of listening to the sermon, I'd watch them through a clear section of the stained-glass window, fluttering and chattering at the big martin house next door. Do you remember them?"

Chris shakes her head. "Not really, but someone in the neighborhood must still have martin houses."

A bird swoops down to snatch a bug in front of the church marquee. It reads: Easter Sunday Worship Service 10:30 AM.

"Did you hear Janet ask us to stay and go to church with them in Fowler?" I say. "I think she said everyone else is staying."

"Yeah." Chris nods. "She wants to fill a pew with cousins. Janet knows we're starting back home, though. No one else has to drive as far as we do. I don't want to drive in the dark."

"And I don't want the expense of another night in

the hotel. I'm saving for our October trip to Galveston." I look at the sign and feel a twinge of regret that we didn't plan to stay another day. "Kind of ironic, isn't it? We hardly ever miss a Sunday, but we're skipping church on Easter."

Chris looks at me and smiles. "I didn't pack anything dressy, anyway."

"I wonder if the women still all wear dresses to church here?"

She gives me a crooked grin. "It may feel like we're in a time warp, but I'm sure Quincy isn't as provincial as it was when we were kids. You did notice the satellite dish on our old house?"

I smile. "I guess a new frilly dress every Easter is not mandatory anymore."

Chris laughs. "They didn't check with Mama when they relaxed that rule." She signals and pulls away from the curb.

"No one messed with Mama's traditions. She always did holidays right, probably because her parents didn't... or couldn't." I close my eyes for a moment, remembering. "We got a new dress to wear on Easter Sunday, whether or not we wanted it."

"What do you mean? Who wouldn't want a new dress?"

I laugh. "That would be me—at least not one year."

"When was that?"

"I think it would have been '56 or '57. Ultra feminine was the fashion—hour glass, you know. That wasn't me."

## New Dress
## Mid-1950s

In the changing room at Block & Kuhl, my mother zipped up the back of the bright blue dress. The fabric was too stiff, the skirt too full, and the tailored bodice scratchy. But at least it wasn't ruffled like the last one she insisted I try on.

"It feels crispy," I said.

"That's 'cause it's taffeta." Mama turned me around to admire the front. She smoothed out the skirt. "See how it stays nice and full. Looks so rich." Mama often favored things she thought wealthy folks might like. I stuck out my bottom lip as I looked down at the shiny fabric.

Mama's eyes brightened. "And it's on sale. Imagine that—right before Easter."

Shopping for a new dress wasn't optional. All three of us kids got new clothes for Easter—period. New dresses drew attention, and I preferred to blend in. I was fourteen, an inch shorter than my younger sister, and still as flat-chested as I was at age six. More than anything in the world, I wanted curves like the other girls my age. I liked a boy in my Sunday school class. Kenny Schmitt was lean and tall, with a lopsided smile and mesmerizing eyes. He would never pay attention to a girl who still looked like a kid. A glossy new dress wouldn't make me look grown up. It would just highlight my defects. Breasts. I needed breasts!

While I tried on the dress, my sister waited out by the three-way mirrors. Her new dress, a frilly pink affair with a big bow at the waist, lay folded and wrapped in tissue paper inside a JCPenney shopping bag.

Chris had chosen the second dress she tried on, but I refused everything Mama had suggested. She vetoed the only one I liked, a soft-green, A-line with a Peter Pan collar that hadn't accented my inadequacy.

"Too plain and juvenile," Mama had said. I didn't even get to try it on.

I frowned at my reflection in the changing room mirror. "Too fancy," I said. "Why can't I get the green one I liked at Penney's."

"Would you quit it with that dress," Mama said, a sharp edge to her voice. "It wasn't for a young lady —and it was way too ordinary for Easter." She pinched her lips and gave me a look that said I better stop complaining. "I don't have all day."

My stomach clenched.

"Get out there and look at yourself in the big mirror." Mama pushed me through the curtain. "It's a very pretty dress and it looks nice on you."

The girl in the three-way mirror disagreed. The bodice, constructed to fit snugly, did—everywhere but where my breasts were supposed to be. I took a deep breath and pushed out my chest. It didn't help —I looked ridiculous. I'd be even more conspicuous in shiny blue.

All the girls in my grade at school wore bras. Even my sister's figure was developing faster than mine, and she was a whole year younger! What was wrong with me? At this rate, I would never become a woman.

I mentioned my concern to Mama once.

"Quit being so foolish," she'd said. "It's a waste of time to worry about such things. It'll happen—just wait and see."

"Let's go home, please," I begged. "I don't need a new dress. I can wear my purple one."

My mother ignored me. "Blue is a nice color on you—bright and cheery."

"I like my new dress, Mama," Chris said.

My sister wasn't helping. Our eyes met, and I stuck out my tongue at her.

Mama stood behind me as I faced the mirror. She smiled, but it didn't reach all the way to her eyes. If I read her expression right, she thought it wasn't great but was the best we were likely to do. She wasn't going home without a new Easter dress for us both.

Mama and her four siblings had grown up with hand-me-downs. Never had a new dress, not even for Easter. She had gone without, always wanting what she couldn't have. Food for holiday dinners came in charity baskets from the local Christian church. If her father was home when the church ladies came, he rejected their gifts. He'd call them "do-gooders" and send them away.

Although we lived on the poor side of town, Mama made sure we weren't neglected or deprived. Our family went to church like 'respectable' folks. Come Easter, Mama fixed a ham for dinner, and my brother, sister, and I got Easter baskets filled with chocolate eggs and candy—and we wore new clothes to church.

Tears rose as I looked at myself in the department store mirror. Why couldn't Mama see how humiliating it was? Didn't she notice I didn't fill out the bodice? I crossed my arms over my chest. "I don't want an Easter dress. Please, Mama. I just want to go home." Tears rolled down my cheeks. I couldn't stop them.

She sighed. "Go change back into your clothes now, and we'll go home. We're all getting tired."

I pulled on my skirt and buttoned up the shirt while my mother gathered up the dresses and left. When I came out of the changing room, she was paying the sales clerk for the blue dress. My heart sank.

"I don't want that dress, Mama!" I stamped my foot in frustration.

Chris grinned at me. "I liked it."

I glared at my sister.

"That's quite enough, young lady." Mama narrowed her eyes and pointed at me. "You're both getting new Easter dresses. That's all there is to it." She clicked her pocketbook closed and said with a softer tone, "It's a pretty dress, Alice. You're just tired."

The clerk handed her the shopping bag and Mama said to us, "Now come on. If we hurry, we can catch the three o'clock bus."

I sat cold and silent as the bus bounced down Eighth Street toward home. Chris chattered away about her new pink dress. "It's just perfect," she said. "What did you say the bow was made of,

Mama?"

"It's satin, honey." Mama smiled at Chris. "That's why it has that pretty sheen." She glanced at me. "You girls are both going to look darling on Easter, like little ladies."

I could hardly swallow past the lump in my throat. I was doomed. There was no escaping it. I'd have to wear that showy new dress on Sunday.


On Easter morning I put on the cruel blue dress and stood in front of the mirror. It was fashioned to fit a woman's body, not mine. Everyone would see me in church and snicker, including Kenny Schmitt. Betty Zimmerman was sure to give me an uppity look. She had bosoms as big as Mrs. Ludwig and bounced them around like some kind of movie star. I wasn't jealous—all I wanted was to look like a regular fourteen-year-old girl.

I tried stuffing Kleenex to fill out the scrunched up places where my breasts should be. But the wads of tissue kept slipping down and looked silly. It would be so much worse than even gym class. There, I could at least hide my deficiency behind my gym locker door when we dressed. Tears streamed down my cheeks.

Everyone at church would know I was some freak

of nature. The crumpled taffeta over my flat chest would scream to the world, "Look! Alice is not normal." There would be nowhere I could hide, no way to disguise my shame.

If I told Mama the dress made me feel sick inside, she would just tell me I was being foolish again.

"Let's go," Daddy called through the house. "We're going to be late for Sunday school."

I dried my tears, pasted on a smile and walked to the car, the dress swishing around my knees.

Daddy smiled as we climbed in the car. "You're a colorful pair today."

David, in a new shirt and trousers, crowded beside us in the back seat, loosening his tie.

Mama wore a new patterned scarf with her best blouse, and sat up straight in the front seat with Daddy, who sported a new tie, too. "Everyone looks nice today," Mama said. "Happy spring colors. That's the way it should be at Easter."

When I walked into Sunday school, I felt like everyone stared at me. Kenny Schmitt was there, and so was Betty Zimmerman. I clutched my Bible over my chest and hurried to the back row, my full skirt rustling as I took a seat. Mrs. Krause told us the story of the miracle when God raised Jesus from his grave. She told us God loved us and always listened to our prayers. I wasn't sure God cared how I looked in my new dress, but just in case, I prayed that he'd make everybody not look at me today.

During the church service, I folded my arms across my chest to hide the collapsed fabric over my nipples, wishing I could sink into the pew and become invisible.

Mama leaned toward me and whispered, "What's wrong, honey? You don't look well."

I looked up, my throat tight and tears rimming my eyes. I said nothing.

She patted my hand.

I'm not sure if God answered my prayer, but no one said anything to me about my dress.

When we got home, Mama said, "Before you change clothes, kids, get your baskets and let Daddy take your picture."

My shoulders sagged, but while Mama fixed dinner, we went in the backyard where Daddy lined us up. I stood pigeon-toed, holding my Easter basket over my chest and frowned.

"Say cheese," Daddy said, and the camera clicked.

# April, 2019, Saturday, Late Afternoon

"I think I remember that picture." Chris says. "My hip is sort of cocked out, and we're all holding our Easter baskets?"
"That's the one. And you are the only one smiling. Every time I look at that photo now, I see the pain in my eyes."

"How sad."

"I never wore that dress again. I'm not sure why Mama didn't make me. It wasn't like her to waste money on a dress that only got worn once. She must have realized at some point how unhappy it made me feel."

"Maybe that was God answering your prayer."

"I think maybe it was."

We sit in companionable silence for a while outside the church. Then Chris speaks. "Want to see if it's unlocked and go inside?"

"Not really, I don't want to explain our presence if we meet someone."

"Wouldn't you like to see if the baptistery mural is still there?"

"I can't imagine it would be. I painted it over forty years ago." Actually, I didn't want to see it painted over, which was surely the case. Or worse—if it was still there—cringe at the realization that it wasn't as good as I once thought.

"That was really something when you think about it." She meets my eyes. "How many sixteen-year-olds have been asked to paint a mural in a brand-new sanctuary?"

I shake my head. "I don't know what possessed them to trust a kid with something so huge… and permanent."

"It wasn't like you were a beginner. You won about every art contest you entered."

"If Dolores hadn't been there for me, I wouldn't have known where to begin.

## Miss Hays
## 1950s


Mama enrolled me in a Saturday art class at the local YWCA when I was eight. My whole family knew I loved making pictures. Uncle Alvin worked at the paper mill in town and provided me with a never-ending supply of blank paper. I spent hours in my room drawing with colored pencils, crayons, and chalk.

"You'll learn to paint at the Y," Mama said, "from a real artist."

I bit my fingernail. I'd never met an artist, and the idea of meeting one was both intimidating and exciting.

"So glad you can join us," the teacher said when I arrived for my first lesson. There was nothing flashy or stylish about Dolores Hays. She wore her graying hair in a no-nonsense ponytail and a bib apron wrapped around a simple blouse and skirt. Yet there was an elegance about her that drew me to her immediately.

I managed a shy smile and glanced around the room at the fifteen or so other kids—all close to my age. The room was colorful with unframed pictures tacked to the walls, three rows of sturdy easels, and a sink in the corner. A table along one wall held pencils, jars of paint, rags, paper towels, pads of paper, and brushes standing in fruit jars.

"What's your name?" Miss Hays asked.

"Alice." I didn't meet her eyes.

"Alice," she repeated with a smile in her gentle voice. "I've always loved that name."

Miss Hays rested her hand on a wooden easel with tear-off sheets of paper. "This will be yours." Lined along the built-in tray at the bottom of the easel sat jars of bright-colored paint, a can of water, and a cylinder containing two brushes.

I picked up the larger brush and rotated it in my hand; I'd finger-painted in school but had never held a brush before. I didn't know what I was supposed to do.

"We're just going to have fun today and get to know our materials." She smiled again, her eyes sparkling with encouragement. "We're using tempera paint, and you will clean your brushes in that water." She touched the water jar. "You can paint anything you want. If you have questions, just let me know." She gestured to a boy about my age with blond hair at the easel next to mine. "This is Johnny Fountain. He can help you get started."

"Hi." Johnny blushed, and the corner of his mouth tugged upward. He pointed to the sink. "We get clean water over there when ours gets dirty."

I looked around at the other kids, and at Johnny. Everyone began painting on their paper. I dipped the brush into a jar of blue paint and dragged it like a mop across the top of the paper creating the sky. I brushed some white paint onto the blue, swirling my brush through the wet sky. Then I dabbed in a little purple. The colors blossomed as they mixed on the paper—instantly fascinating me.

"Good, Alice. You're getting the hang of it." Miss Hays said, crossing the room to look. "I love the colors you're blending together."

A whole new world opened up for me on those Saturday afternoons when I held that brush and painted. Miss Hays was the soul of kindness, and generous with her praise, as she was with all the kids, but she made me feel special.

Mama told me that our teacher made her living painting signs and murals and volunteered her time to teach children. Miss Hays became my standard of what it meant to be an artist. I soaked up everything I could from her, eager to learn more.

One day, after several months, Miss Hays asked me to stay after class.

"Alice, I'm starting an evening art class at Chaddock School this week, and wondered if you might like to take it. It's free, and I'd be happy to pick you up and take you home afterwards. I just live a few blocks from you."

"Chaddock?" I frowned. "Isn't that just for boys who got in trouble?"

"A few of them have been in trouble, but mainly it's a boarding school for boys who have difficult family situations. Some don't have parents at all." She tilted her head. "You will be the only girl, but that won't matter. The important part is that I'll be teaching techniques we don't get into at the Y." She raised her brows. "With your talent, I'd like to see you go further. Wouldn't you like that?"

I hesitated. All boys? But the look on Miss Hays' face told me this was a great opportunity. I nodded. "If Mama says it's okay." It seemed odd, but if Miss Hays said it would be all right, I wasn't worried. I hoped my parents would agree. They did.

Under Miss Hay's supervision, I attended the class for the next three or four years. The other students who came and went during that time were nice to me, and even though they were boys, I always felt comfortable.

Miss Hays introduced us to several media—calligraphy, screen printing, monoprints. We experimented with pastels, watercolor, acrylics, collage and charcoal, too.

Not only did Miss Hays provide my transportation, I suspect she paid for my art supplies. I doubt my parents could have afforded them. I don't remember her ever asking for money.

I realize now she wanted me to have those experiences—to give me a glimpse of the possibilities. Dolores Hays was always gracious, warmhearted, and asked nothing in return. She was my teacher, role model, and mentor before I knew the meaning of the word. With her encouragement, I dared to dream of becoming an artist when I grew up.

The summer I turned thirteen, Miss Hays invited me to go on vacation with her to the Ozarks. Her niece and an artist friend of hers went too, and we spent a week in Rockaway Beach. I loved it. We stayed in a cabin on the shores of the White River. Miss Hays and Harriet, her friend, painted the local scenery while Judy and I swam, explored the woods around the cabin, collected clam shells, and played tic-tac-toe in the sand using pebbles and shells instead of Xs and Os.

One afternoon, we spent hours building an elaborate old-west fort on the beach. We collected sticks from the woods and built a fence around it and stuck small leafy branches in the sand for trees.

Back at school, I signed up for every art class offered. I entered poster contests and won first place in the Civic Music Association competition three years in a row. My prize was two season tickets. I was excited to win, but my mother was over the moon. She took me to the concerts.

When I was sixteen, our minister came to our house. It wasn't unusual for Charles Webb to visit. Mama and Daddy helped with the church's youth program, and they had a lot of interaction with our preacher, whom everyone called Chuck. But this time, he came to see me.

Chuck, lanky with a blond crew cut, held out a photograph of a lake with mountains in the background and trees on the far shore. "Do you think you could paint this on a wall at the church? It's for the new baptistery. It would be quite large —about twelve foot wide and almost eight foot high." Our church's new building was almost finished, and they wanted a mural painted above the baptistery where people becoming Christians were immersed.

"Twelve feet?" My voice almost squeaked, and I touched my fingers to my lips, swallowing hard. I couldn't imagine painting anything that big. "I—I don't know." A knot formed in my stomach. It seemed overwhelming to even consider.

Mama smiled. "That's right down your alley, Alice."

Did my mother have something to do with this? She was always volunteering me for things—anything artistic.

"But Mama." I spread my hands a couple feet apart. "I never painted anything bigger than this."

"Here, I'll leave the picture with you," our preacher said, handing me the photograph. "Think about it for a day or so. I have faith you can do it."

Daddy came home from the factory, and I told him about the minister's request. He took the picture and studied it.

I grimaced. "I wouldn't be able to step back and see how it was all working together—not if I'm in the baptistery. There's not enough room. That's important when you are painting, especially something that big. Twelve feet is huge." I shook my head. "I don't think I can do it."

He put his hand on my shoulder. "Sure you can."

"I can't, Daddy, really. I'd have to be a giant to reach the top of the wall, too. There's just too many problems."

"That part's no problem. I'll build some scaffolding for you. Why don't you ask Dolores Hays? She paints murals, doesn't she? She'd be happy to give you some pointers. Didn't she paint that mural on the wall in Deter's? That's bigger than twelve foot."

"But Miss Hays is a professional artist. I'm just sixteen with no experience. They should ask her to paint it."

"Maybe they want a member of our church to do it —somebody everyone at church knows. It will mean more that way." Mama sighed. "You should be excited, Alice. It's a great honor to be asked, and Chuck thinks you will do a good job."

A part of me thought it would be fun to try, but what if it didn't work out? How humiliating to fail at something so—public.

"It won't hurt to ask Dolores what she thinks," Mama said.

Mama and Daddy were so reassuring, I called Miss Hays.

"Of course, you can do it," she said immediately. "And I'll be happy to help you get started. Let's schedule a time for you to come over and we'll talk about it."

She explained how to prepare the wall and prime it, how to enlarge the image by using a grid method, and then transfer it by sections to the wall. She suggested the paints and brushes to use and answered all my questions.

"You have a good eye for color. It will just be a matter of copying each area of the grid, one at a time. Then you won't have to go back often to see the whole image. You'll do a great job!"

The butterflies in my stomach faded with her praise. "Can I call you if I run into trouble?"

"Absolutely, anytime. We'll work out any problems you have."

On the following Friday evening, my father took me to buy the paint and other supplies, which the church paid for. He rigged up a moveable platform for me to stand on while I painted. The next morning I laid out the grid with string and chalk the way Deloris suggested and began sketching the lake scene in the picture. Just sketching it took the whole of Saturday and Sunday afternoon. Once I got started, the excitement carried me on. I worked on the mural every day after school, and weekends over the next three weeks.

After I laid down the last brush stroke, I walked halfway down the center aisle in the sanctuary. I turned and looked back. Yes! The mountains, the trees, the water. It all looked right together— peaceful. I sighed, a warmth spreading through me. I wouldn't have to be embarrassed.

Compliments and praise from church members poured in. My parents burst with pride when a reporter came out to take a picture of me with the mural for a writeup in a magazine.

When Dolores came to see it, she gave me a hug. "I knew you could do it, Alice. It's lovely. The colors are… perfect." That was the best praise of all.

## April, 2019, Saturday Evening

"Did you ever see Miss Hays again after you went off to college?" Chris asks.

"Just once. I went to see her when I stayed overnight in Quincy on my way to an art show in Chicago. She was still living on Adams Street with her sister, and she was as gracious as ever. It was sad, though. She was nearly blind by then, and her sister had to help her get around. We sat on her porch, drank iced tea and talked. It pleased her I was working as an artist." I sigh. "That had to be thirty years ago."

"She probably passed away a long time ago."

"I was lucky to know her. I'm sure I wouldn't have had a career as an artist without Deloris."

Chris checks the time. "Do you have the address of the Sprouts Restaurant? We're supposed to meet them there in a few minutes."

A pleasant breeze sweeps over me almost four

hours later as I wave goodbye to our cousins. We walk across the restaurant parking lot, and I stoop to get into Chris's car. "Gosh, that was fun," I say, glancing up through the windshield at the full moon, bright in the evening sky.

"Can you believe we were there for so long?" Chris pulls to the exit and waits for traffic to clear.

We'd spent the last hours seated around a long table at Sprouts with eight family members.

Chris turns left and heads south. "That Janet is a character."

Janet is only fifty-six—born to Aunt Emma in her late thirties, the same year I had my first child. She's by far the most outgoing of us all. Janet is also the repository of our family stories.

"The minute she got there, she was holding court." I smile.

I roll down my side window to let in some air. "I didn't expect to enjoy myself nearly as much— when you consider that at least half of us are quiet by nature."

Early into our meal, Janet had related a story or two that cast her mother in an unflattering light, but they were told with such humor that it was infectious. Before long we were all sharing memories of the quirks and foibles of our less-than-perfect family.

"I never heard some of those tales before." Chris turns right at the corner and heads toward our hotel. "I think Aunt Maxine and Emma would have been aghast at our dinner conversation. I know Mama would have."

"Yeah, there's no way she'd approve of us 'airing dirty laundry' in public—even to kin." I smile at Chris. "It was funny laundry, though, and really, all the stories were told with affection."

We had lingered over coffee after the meal, laughing, talking, not wanting to break the spell. A warm flush of tenderness for my cousins rippled through me. They're good people who enjoy life and care for one another. Most of us are getting on in years and have had our own struggles and heartaches. We've made mistakes and learned from them. We were raised by parents who had little in the way of role models, yet with faith and love, they instilled good values in us.

Chris slows the car to a stop at a light. "It's no wonder Mama and her sisters had a few kinks—when you consider they grew up in Grandpa Harry's house."

Grandpa resembled a tall, broad-shouldered Swede, but was mostly German. He was probably handsome when he was young, but I remember a face with deep lines and grim eyes.

"I'm sure Grandpa would have justified the way he was—rationalized all the things he did and didn't do." I rub the back of my neck, trying to work the stiffness out. "If I looked hard, I might find reasons for some of his failings."

"Really?" Chris catches my eye for a second. "I've never heard anyone else make excuses for him."

"From what I heard, his drinking didn't start until he lost his job during the Great Depression. He'd been close to being certified as a plumber."

"It's still no excuse." Chris shook her head. "Lots of people lost their jobs without becoming abusive drunks."

"I've always suspected he had a genetic predisposition—you know, for mental illness. It's not like we haven't had several family members diagnosed with serious mental disorders," I remind Chris. "I'm not saying it justified the beatings—or the neglect—but things are rarely all black-and-white."

"It might be easier to excuse him if his family hadn't suffered so much." Chris pulls into the Holiday Inn parking lot and turns off the engine. We sit and talk for a while.

"I'm just being the devil's advocate. I know the

hell he put Grandma Edna through—all those pregnancies, all those losses, all the deprivation."

Grandma had the high cheekbones of her Native American grandmother. I remember her as quiet, kind, and beaten down by life—and often ill. My mother, being the oldest, assumed many of the household responsibilities before her teens— cooking and cleaning. From what I'd been told, the older kids cared for the younger ones with little support from the adults in the family."

Mama told stories of rarely having enough of anything for the large family. Clothes came from charity boxes, and were passed down to the younger children until they were rags. They nearly froze in the Illinois winters because there wasn't money to keep the house warm. To help feed the family, Mama collected used grease from a restaurant to make gravy. They learned to make do with very little.

She told me once when she was old—and less guarded—that her father came to her bed drunk once and tried to force himself on her. She fought him off and told him if he ever tried it again, or with one of her sisters, she'd kill him. Mama said she meant it, too. As far as she knew he never bothered her or her sisters like that again. The story is told that Grandma cut him off after the twelfth child—seven of them dead. He had girlfriends, Janet said, but she stayed with him until her death.

Mama told me once Grandpa Harry quit drinking and moved the family to Missouri to work on a farm when she was in high school. They had enough to eat for a while, and the children even went to church. But it didn't last long. The drinking began again and so did the beatings.

Grandma took the brunt of the abuse—physical and verbal—and when she died at 57, she looked twenty years older.

"I honestly don't have that many memories of Grandpa—or Grandma," Chris says.

"I don't have many either. Most of what I know is what Aunt Emma told Janet. Mama didn't want us kids around him when he was drinking, so we rarely visited them."

A car parks beside us and a family gets out.

I wait to speak until they walk toward the lobby. "I remember him cursing and barking orders at Grandma. With his temper, Mama always worried about what he might do."

"But it's not like Mama never got mad herself. I saw her lose it more than once. Daddy had a temper, too, we just didn't see it often."

I chuckle. "Just enough that we were afraid to

cross either of them."

"You know," Chris catches my eye. "Mama got so mad at me once, she threw a saucer at me."

I almost choke. "Honestly? I can't imagine that. I don't think I remember her ever being mad enough to throw something. For heaven's sake, what had you done?"

"I can't remember what started it, but she and I were in the kitchen and I said—or did—something that set her off, and she hurled the saucer in her hand at me." Chris touches her nose with her palm. "Hit me square in the face and bloodied my nose."

I snicker. "I know it's not funny… but it is—sort of. I can't quite picture Mama doing that."

Chris laughs, too. "That's not the funny part. There I was bleeding on the kitchen floor, and Daddy chose that instant to come home from work."

"What happened?"

"That's what Daddy asked—and before I could answer, Mama said, 'She walked into the door.' Of course, I wasn't about to dispute her story."

"That's incredible. Mama lied to him? Right in front of you?"

"Yep. Our always-tell-the-truth Mama."

"Well, it's not like she was a saint." I chuckle again.

We roll up the car windows and walk to the lobby entrance. "I guess the fact that an incident like that stands out so much is because it was so rare," Chris says as we let ourselves into our hotel room, "and so out of character."

"I only remember one time when Mama lost it." I set my purse on the dresser and sprawl on the bed. "But thank goodness, it wasn't for anything I'd done. I'm not sure David or you were there, but I think you probably were."

## Grandma Edna's Dresses
## Late-1950s

It happened the spring I turned sixteen. I went into the kitchen to get the last piece of my birthday cake. Mama had just answered the phone.

"Gone? What do you mean she's gone?" Mama slumped onto a chair. Her hand shook and her face was as white as a bedsheet. "Dead?"

Grandma had died on the way to the hospital. "She couldn't get her breath," Mama told me as tears streamed down her face. She covered her eyes with one hand and held up her other palm, as if to stop me from approaching.

I didn't know what to say or do, anyway, and just stood there with my mouth open, suddenly chilled to my bones. She seemed beyond comfort and went to her bedroom to cry alone.

Daddy and Mama took us to the funeral home to say goodbye to Grandma Edna the evening before they buried her. The only dead person I'd seen had been on television. I really didn't have a relationship with my Grandma since I hardly ever saw her, and I was curious more than anything.

Mama talked to Daddy in the front seat on the way. "I hope she looks like she's sleeping—at peace. I keep thinking about her struggling to breathe." Her voice was strangled. "That's not the memory I want to keep."

Gloomy music was playing when we got to the funeral home. The scene seemed surreal like in a movie. A somber man in a black suit took us to a room that smelled like flowers. Aunt Emma and some of my cousins were already there. Everyone talked quietly, and no one smiled.

Mama looked at her mother in the casket. She touched her face and whimpered some words I couldn't make out. My stomach ached, and I felt bad for her. Daddy put his arm around Mama.

I hardly recognized Grandma Edna. She didn't look real. The waxy-faced woman in the coffin didn't look like anyone I remembered at all. I tried to think about when she was alive. Grandma had been nice and hugged me, but I didn't really know her.

Chris touched her. I didn't want to—just wanted to go home.

Aunt Maxine cried real loud and hugged Grandma's body in the casket. I could tell by

Mama's face she didn't think that was proper.

I sat in an upholstered loveseat with my sister as my relatives talked. David and my young cousins all sat quietly, too. Occasionally, someone stood and looked at Grandma's body for a bit, wiping tears, and speaking to her like she could hear. We stayed all evening. Grandpa Harry never came, and hardly anyone did that wasn't related.

Our parents didn't insist that we go with them to the funeral service the next morning. All three of us kids elected to not go. We stayed home and ate streusel coffee cake that Marie had brought over when she heard about Grandma dying.

Mama cried most all the time that week, her eyes red and puffy even when she wasn't crying.

A month or two after Grandma Edna died, Mama found out that Grandpa had already married some woman he knew. When she cooked supper that night, she mumbled under her breath and slammed cabinet doors and drawers. "That man doesn't have a shred of decency! Mama's barely cold, and he's got himself another wife!"

The next evening, after Daddy came home from work, he took Mama to Grandma's house to collect some of her things. She didn't want his new woman to have them, and she and my aunts would have something to remember Grandma Edna by.

Mama stomped into our house afterwards, carrying only a few dresses, and tossed them onto the sofa. "He probably sold anything he thought he could get a little money for," she said. "He never cared about Mama or he wouldn't have treated her like dirt."

Grandpa showed up at our house the next afternoon when Daddy was at the factory. Mama and I were in the kitchen. It's the only time I remember him coming to our house.

"You're a damn thief," he hollered at Mama. "Comin' to my place when I was out and helping yourself. I knowed it was you. I never said you could take them clothes."

"Go home, Daddy. You're drunk!" Mama waved a hand at him. "Get out of my house. I don't want you around my kids."

"Give me what's mine, and I'll go." He sounded strange, slurring his words.

Mama put her hands on her hips and took a big breath. "Those dresses were Mama's, not yours. You'd just give them to that hussy you married."

"Damn you, Lola." He raked his hand through his gray hair. "Ain't none of your business what I do with them. You give me them clothes or I'll sic the law on you for stealing what belongs to me." He pointed a finger at Mama. "I know people."

I never saw Mama look so mean. Her face turned red, and she scrunched her eyes. "I'm not afraid of you or your ole drinking buddies. Now get out! I never want to see you again as long as I live!"

Grandpa lifted a hand as if to hit Mama, glaring at her with a face as red as a beet. "You just wait." He shook a fist at Mama. "I'll be back with the law." He turned to leave.

Mama screamed, "I'll burn my mama's dresses before I let your whore get her hands on them."

## April, 2019, Saturday Night

"And?" Chris sits up in bed.

"That's exactly what Mama did when Grandpa Harry left. She gathered up Grandma's dresses and burned them in the barrel out back."

Chris's eyes went round. "I remember! Mama out there stuffing her mother's clothes in the barrel and setting them on fire. You'd think I could remember more—I was fourteen." She shrugged. "I doubt Grandpa would have gotten very far with the authorities."

"Me either," I say. "But she wasn't taking any chances. There was no way Mama was going to give her mother's clothes to that man for another woman."

"Do you know if he came back?"

"As far as I knew then, she never saw him again. I never heard anything about him or his new wife until years later when Mama called me in Oklahoma to tell me Grandpa had died. He'd had cancer and she and her sisters had taken care of him in his final days. Families, even dysfunctional ones, are still family.

 Later that night as we lay on our beds in the dark hotel room, Chris asks softly, "Are you asleep?"

"No, why?" I say.

"I've just been thinking. I had a great time tonight, but I feel kind of bad too, 'cause it doesn't feel like we were fair to our parents, all the stories about their flaws and peculiarities."

"Yeah." Chris has a point. "We kind of got carried away. When you think about it, it's amazing Mama turned out the way she did. She was pretty darn strong."

"She didn't have much of a home life when she was growing up, but she and Daddy worked hard to provide a better one for their children. We've got lots of good memories." I hear the smile in Chris's voice. "Like the picnic on the last day of school every year when Mama had a basket all packed, and we'd go to the park, just us kids and her."

A sliver of light comes through the drapes from the parking lot as I remember. "And how about the gingerbread Mama always made on the first day it snowed? We'd eat it warm from the oven with butter."

She wasn't perfect, but Mama gave us something powerful she didn't have when she grew up. We always felt loved and protected.

We lay in the darkness and recount the many little ways our parents made us feel valued—seemingly insignificant in isolation, but together they paint a picture of a caring and supportive family.

## April, 2019, Sunday Morning

I fiddle with the hotel's coffee maker before six the next morning, trying to make a cup without disturbing Chris's slumber. She wakes and is dressing by the time I take my first drink of the weak brew.

"We might as well get an early start since we have so far to drive today." Chris pulls on a red top over her jeans.

"Maybe we could take a different route home— down through the Ozarks instead of picking up I-44 at Cuba? What d'ya think?"

She gives me a thumbs up, her face bright. "You're the navigator. It will be nice to see the lake again."

We check out of the hotel, and as the sun rises, we drive west on Broadway toward the bridge over the Mississippi.

I lower the window to feel the wind on my face as we cross the wide expanse of chocolate-colored water into Missouri. "Goodbye, David—goodbye, Quincy—goodbye, river." Closing my eyes, I can almost feel the cool spray as Daddy opens up the 20 hp Evenrude and we skim across the surface of the river full throttle.

I open my eyes again and look down at the river. "Before I die, I'd like to ride in a fishing boat again down there." A swell of melancholy sweeps over me. "Wouldn't be the same without Daddy, of course. What I wouldn't give to run a trotline in the backwaters with him one more time."

"You okay?" Chris draws her eyebrows together. "You're not sounding like yourself."

"It's just… being in Quincy. We've been immersing ourselves in memories. And it's hitting me that memories are so…" I search for the word. "Intangible—all that's left of the past—of a big part of our lives. Things are all slipping away."

"I guess everything slips away eventually." Chris smiles sadly. "You can't let it get you down."

"I don't mind so much getting old. I just thought it would take longer."

Chris chuckles. As we drive through the gently rolling countryside, we listen for an hour or more to a collection of hymns Janet gave us, singing along to the ones we know. Dogwoods and redbud trees bloom among the bands of trees between fields, farmhouses and barns. Billowing clouds overhead complete the passing bucolic scene.

By nine o'clock we're well into the Ozarks where Highway 54 winds its way through the rocky hills of central Missouri.

"Water!" I shout, catching the first glimpse of the lake.

Chris laughs. "I guess you get the quarter."

When we were children, we vacationed at the Lake of the Ozarks many times, and Daddy made a game of giving a quarter to the first kid who spotted the water. The sprawling lake with eleven hundred miles of shoreline resembles a huge dragon on the map.

Chris pulls onto the first scenic outlook and parks the car. We get out and walk to the railing. I catch my breath at the panorama before us. The lake stretches for miles, a dazzling expanse of brilliant blue with great swaths of glittering stars on the water. I am awed once again at the vastness of the labyrinthine shoreline bordered by trees and limestone cliffs.

"I'm glad we came this way." Chris leans on the rail. "Seeing the lake makes me feel young and old at the same time. Know what I mean?"

"I do. In a lot of ways, I feel like the kid I was sixty years ago when we first came here. That kid is still in me, but it's like a distant dream too—so many changes in my life during those years, so many losses." I snap of few photos of the lake glistening in the sunlight.

Another car parks beside ours and an elderly couple get out. We nod hello and they stand a few feet away and look out over the scene.

Chris turns to the couple. "Beautiful, isn't it?"

The man appears uncertain if her comment was directed at them. He nods. "Sure is." A few moments later, he turns to Chris. "Say, you don't happen to know how far it is to Joplin, do you? We left our map at the cafe where we ate breakfast."

"I don't know off the top of my head, but just a sec and I can tell you." Chris takes a few steps back to her car and fishes out a map from her glove compartment. She hands it to the man. "Here's a map of Missouri. You can keep it."

The man smiles. "We sure appreciate it." He unfolds the map.

"Where you all from?" Chris carries on a conversation with them for a few minutes, telling them how we vacationed at the lake many times when we were kids.

I see our dad in my sister so often, and this is one of those times. That's exactly what he would have done.

"Thanks again for the map," the petite gray-haired woman says as they turn to leave. They both wave as they drive away.

We get back in the car, and Chris pulls back on the highway.

"I don't know how old I was when we came to the lake the first time." Chris checks the traffic in the mirror and accelerates. "Do you remember?"

"I think I was about twelve, maybe a little younger. I know I just finished fifth grade." I lay a hand across my breastbone. "It was love at first sight."

## Lake of the Ozarks
## Mid-1950s

After school let out in June, Daddy drove us to the lake for a two-week stay at the state park. We pulled our fishing boat behind our five-year-old Dodge Coronet, packed with our gear and covered with a tarpaulin. Our family always camped on our summer vacations, often near a stream, and I looked forward to our trips all year.

Daddy gave Chris the quarter several miles back for glimpsing the lake first as we drove on a winding road looking for the park with the campground. We had never been to the Lake of the Ozarks before.

"There's the sign," David pointed out the windshield to the park entrance.

The shimmering blue lake beckoned beyond the tree-lined road. "When can we go swimming?" I asked.

"Yeah," Chris chimed in. "The lake sparkles more than the river."

"We have to get settled in first," Mama said. "It took longer to get here than it should have"—she gave a sideways glance at Daddy—"so maybe not until tomorrow."

When we'd stopped at a road-side park to eat a picnic lunch, Daddy had gotten into a lengthy discussion with a man with long, straggly hair wearing a backpack. That was just Daddy's way, and it often meant we were delayed. Mama never fussed at him about it, but once in a while, she got in a little dig that either went over his head or he ignored.

Daddy drove slowly through the campground looking for our campsite. "There it is." He pointed to a spot with a picnic table surrounded by tall pine trees.

We piled out and watched as Daddy backed the boat trailer into place.

A silver RV with a patio-sized awning sat parked in the spot next to ours. A man, sitting in a lawn chair holding a beer waved hello. We waved back.

"David, help me get the tarpaulin off our gear," Daddy said. "You girls can help unload."

"That guy's lucky." David removed a bungee cord securing the bags and equipment and unhooked another. "All he has to do is park the trailer, and he's finished."

"That's not really camping, son." Daddy pulled off the tarp and folded it. "He's missing half the adventure."

"You girls collect some of those pinecones." He pointed around at the cones scattered all over the campsite. "They'll make good tinder for our campfires."

"These are bigger than the ones at home," Chris said, as we gathered up a bunch of the pinecones while Mama and Daddy surveyed the area and discussed where to position the tents.

When the decisions had been made, David helped Daddy erect our sleeping tents—one for Chris and me, one for our parents, and a pup tent for David.

"You girls start putting up your cots," Mama said when Daddy laid the bundled army cots next to our tent.

David and Daddy erected a big tent over the picnic table so we'd always have a dry place to eat. Mama cooked most of our meals over a campfire, but if it rained, she made do with a little portable Coleman stove under the tent.

With Mama's help, they had things set up and tied down by the time Chris and I struggled with the last wooden posts to put our cots together. Daddy had to help us stretch the canvas to get the end sticks in place.

After we put our army cots in our tent and spread blankets over them, we all stood back and looked at our impressive campsite.

"All the comforts of home." Daddy turned to David. "And without a fancy trailer." When he'd secured our home-away-from-home, Daddy said, "Let's go exploring." He looked at Mama. "You comin', Lola?"

"You guys go along." Mama said. "I'm going to organize our food supplies and start dinner. Otherwise, we won't be eating until dark." She looked up. "Oh, before you go, Bob, start a fire for me, would you?" She pointed to the circle of rocks lined with gray ashes. "I'll cook potatoes with smoked sausage for supper."

Mama sat in a lawn chair with a bowl in her lap and peeled potatoes as David, Chris, and I helped gather dry branches for kindling. Daddy put a pile of our pinecones and smaller twigs in the middle of the fire pit, added some kindling we gathered, and then a few bigger logs that were left nearby. Before long, the fire blazed.

The four of us strolled along the road through the camping area. "That's where we'll be taking our showers," Daddy said, pointing to a little grey building. "And where you'll go to use the bathroom."

I pulled on my dad's shirttail. "Where can we swim?"

"I guess that's as good a place as any to start." Daddy unfolded a map of the park and rotated it, glancing around at the lay of the land. "According to this, the swimming beach is just through there." He pointed to a stand of trees. "There's probably a trail that cuts through. Taking the road is the long way around."

"I'll find it, Daddy." David ran ahead looking for the trailhead. "This might be it," he called out, and then waited for us to catch up.

The path was narrow, but Daddy said it looked like it headed in the right direction.

We started down the shortcut through the woods. "Watch your step, kids." Daddy motioned toward roots protruding from the ground.

The air was cooler under the canopy of trees. Dappled sunlight danced on the forest floor as a breeze rustled the green foliage overhead. Fallen tree trunks lay decaying beside saplings and mature oaks, silver maple, and sweetgum trees. Daddy knew all their names.

"Ah, here's a shagbark hickory." He patted the

trunk of a tree. "See the long, curled strips on the bark? And the leaves on this one. Anyone know what it is?"

"Elm," David said, "like the one in our backyard."

Daddy stopped suddenly and held up his hand. "Look through there." He pointed, his voice scarcely more than a whisper. "See the deer? Look to her right about ten feet, there's a fawn with her."

I sucked in a breath and held it. The doe froze and looked at us for a few moments, then turned. Her white tail flashed as she jumped into the brush with her baby behind her.

We walked a little farther, and I heard a knocking sound. David pointed to a nearby tree trunk where a woodpecker hammered at the bark, its brilliant-red crest ablur.

"It's hunting for bugs," he said.

Chris shrunk back as a bumblebee buzzed passed her. "I don't like bugs."

"Bees won't bother you if you don't bother them," Daddy said as we came to a clearing in the woods with brush no taller than me.

"Blackberry brambles," Daddy said, a twinkle in his eye. He picked a deep-purple berry off a thorny bush and plopped it into his mouth. "We need to remember where these are."

"I didn't know they grew wild." I said, pulling one off the bush and plopping the sweet morsel into my mouth.

We saw three wild turkeys and several squirrels before we got to the end of the trail that opened onto another road.

"There it is." Daddy pointed across the road. A wide blue lake sparkled in the afternoon sun almost to the horizon. At the distant shore, a shimmering reflection of the trees and rocky bank extended into the water.

"Wow," I said. "I never saw so much water." It was wider than the Mississippi River that cut a huge swath through the landscape at home. This lake dwarfed any of the bodies of water I'd ever seen.

A small green shower hut stood in the middle of a grassy area. Beyond that, a retaining wall with massive stone steps led down to a sandy beach at least a hundred feet wide. A boathouse sat at the water's edge at one end of the beach, opposite a rocky shore with pine trees near the water.

Several people swam in the lake. A lifeguard sitting in an elevated wooden chair leaned down to talk to a girl wearing a skimpy swimsuit.

We strolled through the grass and down the steps to the beach. Chris and I took off our flip flops. We ran to the water and laughed as it washed over our bare feet. I picked up a piece of blue glass, smooth and almost round. When I held it up to Chris, it glistened in the sun. I ran back to show it to David, who was examining a clamshell.

"It must be really old to be that smooth," he said.

Kid's laughing voices caught my attention, and I pointed to a dock floating on several steel barrels about eighty feet from the shore. "That looks like fun," I said, watching the kids jumping off, squealing and splashing.

"I'm going to swim out there when we come tomorrow," David said.

I raised up on my toes and looked back at Daddy. "Can we go out there tomorrow?"

"Sure," he said. "Just don't swim out alone. It's a long way."

All three of us kids were strong swimmers. We'd learned at the Y, and swam every summer at the municipal pool a mile from our house and on many weekends in the river with our folks.

Daddy sat on the stone steps while we explored the beach. After half an hour or so, he whistled for us. "Your mother should have our supper ready by now. We better get back."

"Hey, look at this turtle," I said on our return through the woods. I picked up the dome-shaped shell and showed it to the others. The turtle had drawn in with his hinged bottom shell closed tightly.

Chris inspected my find. "Shouldn't he be in the water?"

"That's a box turtle," David said. "They live on land."

"Can I keep him?" I asked Daddy. "I could name him Thomas."

He raised his brows. "I think he'd be happier where you found him."

"Please, Daddy? I really, really want him."

"What you really, really want is not always the right thing."

I reluctantly returned the turtle, patting his shell. "Bye, Thomas."

Daddy stopped along the trail and grabbed the end of a thick dead branch. He broke it easily with his foot. "This'll be nice for our next fire."

We all got into the spirit of it and picked up dry

wood for our next campfire, a practice we would continue every time we headed back.

The smell of sausage and smoke greeted us as we walked into camp with our arms loaded. We piled the wood next to the fire pit. Mama had set the picnic table. We spooned our supper from the cast-iron dutch oven nestled in the coals. It tasted even better than it smelled.

After we finished supper, Daddy put more wood on the fire and we sat in lawn chairs around it as night fell. I gazed up at the dark sky full of flickering stars, excited about swimming in that blue lake tomorrow. When the flames died down, we toasted marshmallows over the glowing embers.

The next morning rain pattered on the canvas roof. My heart sank. "No," I groaned. I shook Chris awake. "There goes swimming today."

She rubbed her eyes and unzipped the tent door, drawing the flap open. "Cats and dogs!" She scrunched up her face. "Maybe it'll quit."

We dressed and ran to the shelter of the cook tent. David and Daddy were sitting at the picnic table, and Mama was making oatmeal on the Coleman stove.

"I don't know why it had to rain today," I complained, in a sour mood.

"Yeah," Chris echoed. "We wanna swim."

"The farmers need the moisture, and you'll have plenty of time to swim. We have two weeks here." Daddy studied a road map unfolded on the table. "It doesn't rain inside caves. We could go see Bridal Cave down by Camdenton."

"You know what lives in caves, don't you?" My brother wore a mischievous grin. "Bats. Millions of bats."

"David!" Mama glared at him.

"I'm not afraid of bats." I crossed my arms over my chest and stuck out my chin. I had touched a fruit bat once that our neighbor Joey found—but millions? I pictured them flying into my hair and getting tangled in it.

Chris's eyes got big. "I don't like bats."

Mama looked at Chris. "Don't worry. Your brother's just trying to scare you. I bet we won't see any bats at all."

I was dubious, but it wasn't up to me or Chris. Daddy decided we would tour Bridal Cave.

It took us over an hour to get there because Daddy

stopped to give a man a ride who was carrying a red gas can in the rain. Chris sat on Mama's lap in the front passenger seat and the wet man squeezed in with David and me. He was nice, but he smelled, and I couldn't get far enough from him to not get wet.

"I sure do appreciate you folks," the man said, after we'd taken him to the nearest exit with a gas station, and transported him back to his car with his can of gas. "Can I pay you something for your trouble?"

"No." Daddy waved him off. "Just pass it along to the next guy you see who needs help."

"I surely will." He saluted Daddy like a soldier. "Thanks again."

## April, 2019, Sunday

Chris laughs as we drive southwest on Highway 54 toward Oklahoma. "That was Daddy. He was always ready to help someone."

I shake my head, smiling. "And talk their ear off when he was doing it. I can't begin to count how many times we sat in the car waiting for Daddy while he talked with someone he was helping, or just talking to some stranger." I glance over at Chris in the driver's seat. "Gee. I wonder who else we know like that."

She grins. "At least I came by it honestly."

"There's a sign for Bridal Cave." I nod toward a billboard as we drive south near Camdenton.

Chris makes a face. "I wasn't crazy about the cave when we went there on our first day at the lake. Were you?"

"No, but mainly because I wanted to go swimming. I guess Daddy thought it was better than waiting around our camp for the rain to stop."

## Character
## Mid-1950s


"Watch out for the bats." David said as we entered the cave.

I stuck out my tongue at him. "Shut up!"

"Behave, kids," Daddy said.

"It's c-c-cold in here." Goosebumps peppered my skin as we stepped into the first big chamber inside the cave. I wrapped my arms around myself and stared up at the giant curtains made of gold-colored rock draped above us—like nothing I'd ever seen.

"Wow. Look at those." Chris pointed at stone icicles hanging from the roof of the cave. Upside-down ones rose from the floor, and some of them touched in the middle and formed huge columns all the way up.

"Bet you don't know those are stalactites and stalagmites," David said in his know-it-all voice.

Chris rolled her eyes.

The tour guide looked at David. "You're a smart young man."

It was my turn to roll my eyes at Chris. I didn't care what they called anything in the cave. I kept thinking about the bats. I shuddered. What if one flew into my hair?

"Do bats live in here?" Chris asked the guide.

He pointed up where it was too dark to see. "Sure. They're roosting from the ceiling."

"They're probably going to poop on your head," David said.

I drew in my shoulders and felt tight in my stomach. "Smart aleck!"

"Shh! Quit fussing and listen," Mama said as our leader began reciting the cave's history.

I didn't much care for the guide. He rambled too much and his jokes were silly.

My mind wandered. The cave was damp and cold and smelled musty. I wanted to be at the beach.

Suddenly, everything went black. Several people gasped. I did too, and reached out for Daddy in the dark, grabbing hold of him.

"Now hold your hand in front of your face," the

guide said. "It's never quite that dark outside, is it?"

I couldn't see anything at all and worried about the bats. "Daddy, I don't like this."

Some of the people laughed. I didn't know if they were laughing at me or they thought it was funny that they couldn't see anything.

Daddy held me close to him. "It's okay. He'll turn on the lights soon enough."

The lights were back on within a minute or two, and we walked along a cement walkway through several other rooms as the guide babbled on. Boring. I wondered when it would be over and hoped the rain had stopped.

I smiled when we exited the cave. The sun shone down from a blue sky filled with puffy white clouds—perfect weather for swimming.

"Yay!" we kids all yelled in unison.

We headed toward the car.

"Oh, no," Mama said. In the parking lot a young man leaned on a car with the hood up. She groaned. "Twice in one day!"

Daddy walked over to the guy. "What's the problem?"

We didn't hear everything they said, but we didn't need to—we all knew Daddy would help. Mama walked to a bench in the shade of a tree and sat down. Chris moaned, and I grumbled and fanned myself with the tour brochure while Dave walked around kicking stones.

Mama took a deep breath. "Just be patient, kids. Your dad is a good man. And sometimes that means you wait."

Daddy and the man leaned over the engine and tinkered with something. Daddy was good at tinkering. Most times, he had people on the road again before long. The man got in the car and tried to start the engine while our dad adjusted something under the hood. After several futile tries, Daddy held up his hand, and the man got out and joined Daddy again.

They repeated this several times until Daddy finally moved our car over next to the man's and attached jumper cables. The guy got in, turned the ignition and the engine roared to life.

The man wore a big smile and pumped Daddy's hand. "Thank you so much. I'm so glad there are people like you."

"Glad to help," Daddy said. "I wouldn't want to live in a world where we don't look out for each other."

Mama smiled when Daddy waved for us to all get in the car.

"Can we swim when we get back to the park?" I asked Mama as I opened the door.

Mama looked at her watch. "It's lunchtime. You can go to the beach after you eat, but you'll have to wait a half hour before you get in the water."

"Oh, Mama," I said. "We already missed half the day."


As soon as we got back to camp, we gobbled down the bologna sandwiches Mama made for us, then changed into our swimsuits.

David grabbed a towel. "Last one there is a rotten egg." He took off running down the path through the woods.

"No fair! He got a head start," Chris said, racing after him.

"Ha ha, I win." David said as I collapsed on the sand.

"That was a dirty trick. You started before we did." The sand stuck to my sweaty legs, and I wanted to wash it off in the water, but spread out my towel instead 'cause Mama had said to wait.

We played in the sand with the warm sunshine on our shoulders, the sound of the lapping waves, and the gulls calling overhead. We built sandcastles and dug holes until we figured our half-hour was up.

"Let's go," Dave shouted, and we dashed into the water, splashing and whooping. I swam toward the floating platform, savoring the feel of water streaming over my body and rushing through my fingers. We climbed up the ladder that extended into the lake. I jumped in the water holding my knees, cannonball style, hitting the surface with an explosion a mile high. It was fun, and I climbed up and did it again.

Other kids were at the dock too—about a dozen—and we all had fun jumping in and seeing who could make the biggest splash. Some of the older kids had a size advantage, but by jumping high and making my body as round as I could, the higher my splash jetted when I hit the water.

A girl screamed when a boy pushed her off the dock and she belly-flopped. The lifeguard blew his whistle and pointed at us.

"I can swim to the shore and back faster than any of you," said Scott, an older boy with a mop of black hair, even under his arms. "That makes me *king of the dock.*"

"Nuh-uh." I shook my head and frowned. I didn't think he looked so fast. "You can't beat *me*."

"Me, neither." My brother puffed out his chest. "I can beat you all."

I was fairly sure my brother could beat Scott. Dave had long legs and was taller than anyone in his class. I wasn't so sure he could out-swim me, though.

I lined up with five other swimmers at the edge of the dock.

A girl with freckles and reddish hair named Susie counted. "At the count of three. One. Two. Three."

We jumped off the dock. I didn't look to see where the others were, and pumped my arms, frog-kicking as fast as I could. I touched the beach with my foot, turned and pushed off, racing back. The return seemed farther as my legs tired. I grabbed the dock and shook the water out of my eyes. Scott was right behind me.

My brother grinned down at us. "Told ya!"

I winced. Now David had something else to brag about. At least I beat that Scott guy.

The other kids laughed and splashed all around us as the others made it back to the dock.

Scott shouted. "The real test of who is *king of the dock* is who can stay under water the longest."

Seven of us lined up in the water with one hand on the dock.

"I'll be the judge again." Susie started counting as we all filled our lungs and ducked under the water.

I held my breath and opened my eyes. I saw the legs of some others and then a little perch swam right past my nose. I wondered what else was in the water with me, but I stayed down until I thought my lungs would burst. I bobbed up.

Susie was saying, "thirty-three." I was the fourth up, Chris told me. By the time Susie counted to fifty, everyone was up but Scott.

She kept counting—all the way to a hundred.

"That's a long time to be underwater," David said. "What if Scott drowns? We better get help."

I stood motionless, my shoulders tight and stomach clenching. Scott could be lying at the bottom of the lake. Everybody looked worried. Chris bit her lip and hugged herself.

David signaled for the lifeguard. He waved that he saw us and came swimming out.

"We were having a contest. Scott hasn't come up,"

David told him.

The sound of my heartbeat thrashed in my ears.

He dove down to search for Scott without saying a word.

We all looked at one another, terrified. One of the younger girls cried. Susie's chin trembled. A boy stood frozen with unblinking eyes; another pressed his fists to the sides of his head. Chris came to stand next to me. I felt her shaking.

The lifeguard popped up, took another breath, and went down again. I held my breath, waiting. After another minute he bobbed to the surface again. A second head appeared.

Scott shook dripping hair out of his eyes and grinned. "I won!"

I let out a huge breath, and my mouth fell open. I hugged Chris—so relieved—and mystified. How did he hold his breath so long?

"I found your friend here under the dock," the lifeguard said, "between the barrels. His head was above water."

"I had you going, didn't I?" Scott said, acting like it was a joke all along.

"Gotta go, Mom's waving at me." Scott dove into

the water and swam to shore.

"I don't like cheaters." I pinched my lips tight.

"Mama says liars and cheaters are as bad as thieves." Chris folded her arms over her chest. "He'll be sorry someday when no one believes him."

Daddy built a roaring fire every evening, and it was one of my favorite times of the day. When the sky was dark, and the fire burned down to coals, we poked marshmallows onto branches and toasted them over the glowing embers. Rotating the branch slowly until they were golden brown and melty inside, we sandwiched the marshmallow and a square of Hershey's chocolate between graham crackers to make s'mores.

One night after we'd been there a week, we sat around our campfire at dusk. The orange and yellow flames twisted around the wood, crackling and sending sparks and smoke upward, and I thought about our wonderful first week at the lake.

Our days had been filled with just having fun outdoors. We fished, picked blackberries, and took long hikes in the woods in the dappled sunlight, explored the winding shore of that huge lake from Daddy's fishing boat, and swam in the welcoming waters of the lake.

When the fire burned down to red-hot coals, I threaded two marshmallows onto my stick and held them over the embers. My marshmallows almost caught on fire when the coals flared as I stared up at the night sky that twinkled with stars.

I had assembled my s'more and taken the first sweet, gooey bite when Daddy cleared his throat. "I thought tomorrow we might go horseback riding. The trail rides start right here in the park."

Chris squealed. "Can we, really?"

My pulse raced. "Can we? Can we?" I hopped up and down, almost dropping my s'more. I'd seen the stables but never dreamed I'd get to ride a horse. The closest I came was when Uncle Wilber let me sit on one when we visited his farm in Iowa. I'd felt like I was on top of the world.

"Unless it rains," Mama said. "It says in the brochure, they don't go on rides when it's muddy."

I looked up at the night sky and mouthed a prayer, "Please God, don't let it rain."

I lay that night on my army-surplus cot, the smell of campfire smoke wafting through the tent flap netting. Insects buzzed, an owl hooted, and roosting birds rustled in the trees. The wind picked up and leaves whispered in the branches. As the night sounds enveloped me, I fell asleep and dreamed of horses.

The next morning Daddy left to run his trotlines as the rest of us emerged from our tent rubbing the sleep from our eyes. The sky was blue with not a cloud in sight.

"I want a fast horse when we go on the trail ride," David said shoveling cereal into his mouth.

"Me too," Chris said as we sat down at the picnic table. "One like Trigger."

Mama offered us blackberries for our cereal. "I'd rather you ride one steady and safe." She swished a fly away. "We don't want a horse running away with you. I think the trail guide will probably choose your horse, anyway."

"I want a friendly one." I remembered Sally, the iceman's horse I used to feed apples to before we had a refrigerator. I closed my eyes, and could almost smell her, feel her velvet-soft nose, and hear her whinny when she wanted more.

"Look what I caught." Daddy held up two blue catfish when he walked into camp. "Dave, you can give me a hand with them." David watched Daddy clean the fish while Chris and I helped Mama clean up from breakfast.

After Daddy filleted the fish and put them in the ice chest, he went to the bathhouse to take a shower.

When he returned, Daddy threw his towel over the line strung up between two trees and turned to Mama. "Do you remember when the first trail ride leaves, Lola? We ought to ride before it gets hot."

"I think nine," Mama said from a lawn chair where she sat sipping coffee.

Daddy gasped. "It's gone!" His voice was shaky and his eyes round. He frantically checked all his pockets. "My wallet. It's gone."

Mama put her hand over her mouth and started to rise. "Are you sure it was with you?"

"It was in my pants pocket," he said, his face contorted and his voice high. "I'm sure of it. It must have fallen out when I got dressed."

Daddy turned and ran back to the shower building. While he was gone, we searched every corner of our campsite, hoping to find it, but it wasn't there. Mama grimaced, looking like it was the end of the world.

He returned to our campsite, his shoulders slumped and all the color drained from his face. "It's not there."

"Oh, Bob." Mama's voice cracked, and she shook her head. "What are we going to do?"

"I don't know. All the money I had was in my wallet—everything except some change."

He sank into a lawn chair and buried his face in his hands while Mama placed her hand on his shoulder. He raised his head looking like he might cry. "I don't have enough to buy gas to go home, let alone this week's groceries." Daddy didn't believe in credit cards. He paid cash and saved for things he wanted.

I wrapped my arms around my stomach and wanted to cry. I chewed on my lip instead.

Mama grabbed her purse and counted the money in her wallet.

"That will get us home, but nothing more," Daddy said and hugged Mama. "I'm sorry, Lola, looks like we have to forget about the last week of our vacation."

Mama's eyes welled with tears, and so did Chris's. The back of my throat began to hurt, but I tried to hold in my distress. We'd been having so much fun. We were even going to ride horses today, and now everything was spoiled. Dave stomped around the campsite and punched a tree.

"Use that energy to help us pack, son," Daddy

said.

Our parents began breaking camp. Mama folded up bedding and put it in storage bags.

As Daddy collapsed an army cot, he paused. "Someone may have found my wallet and turned it in to a ranger or something." Mama stopped too. "Before I pack any more," he said, "I'm going to check at the visitor's center. Maybe they have a lost-and-found. Won't hurt to ask."

"Good idea, Bob," Mama said.

We stopped packing when he went hustling off down the road. Mama smiled at us. "At least you had a fun week. A whole week. When I was a girl, I never ever went on a vacation at all."

It was small consolation. I thought about the horse I wouldn't get to ride. No more swimming and playing out on the dock. I tried to hold back my tears, but I couldn't.

Daddy came back with his mouth pressed in a tight line. "No one turned in a wallet."

David kicked the dirt and Chris teared up again. My insides clenched, and I wanted to scream and bawl, but I didn't want to make Daddy feel worse. I could tell by the way his shoulders sagged that he felt terrible too.

"After you kids pack up your clothes," he said, "scout around the campsite and pick up every piece of trash you find—whether or not we left it —and stack up the wood and kindling by the fire pit. We should leave this place better than when we came."

Daddy loosened the stake on the first tent when a boy of about twelve walked into our campsite. "Are you Mr. Culbertson?" he asked Daddy.

"Yes!" all of us said at the same time. I crossed my fingers and held my breath.

"I found this on the floor in the bathhouse." The boy produced a wallet from behind his back. "I looked at your driver's license. That's how come I knew your name." He handed it to Daddy. "Here. I been looking for you ever since."

Mama clasped her hands together and pressed them to her heart. I let out my breath and hugged Chris. David shouted, "Yay" and danced around. Daddy looked like he'd just escaped a death sentence.

"Oh, thank you, young fella." He opened the wallet and his bills were still there. "You just saved us from having to go home." He held up a hand. "Stay right there." Daddy went into his tent and came out with his binoculars. "Do you have a good pair of binoculars? If not, I'd like you to have these."

The boy said he didn't and took the gift. "Gee, Thanks." He grinned as he looked through the lenses. "Wow. This is great."

After the boy left, Mama looked up. "Thank you, God."

We all began putting things back in our tents. Ten minutes later the same boy came back, binoculars in hand. The man with him frowned.

"My son can't accept your gift. It was kind of you, but he was just doing what's right."

The boy held out the binoculars to Daddy.

Daddy looked at the man. "I really wish you'd let him keep them. He saved us from having to drive home before our vacation had barely begun."

"That may be true but I want my son to learn that doing what is right is reward enough." The man put an arm across the boy's shoulders.

"Did you expect a reward for returning it?" Daddy asked the boy.

"No sir," he said.

"It's not really a reward. I see it as a gift, because every boy should own a good pair of binoculars."

The boy glanced up at his father.

"Really," Daddy said. "Please, let your boy keep the binoculars."

The boy's dad nodded.

Daddy smiled. We all did.

## April, 2019, Sunday

Those relaxed days at the lake were precious
moments. I've loved shorelines my whole life.
Even the fishy smell at the water's edge. Whether
it's a river bank, a sandy beach, or a gentle
gurgling brook—the places where water caresses
land never fail to take me back to those treasured
memories.

They say you can't go home again. The same is
true of vacations. Every golden experience is
unique and never shines quite the same when you
try to recapture it. Reclaiming the past is not what
this trip has been about, however. We've been
saying goodbye.

"It's been nice to go home," Chris says as we drive
toward Oklahoma. "The open house, the old
places, our cousins." Then she adds, almost
mirroring my own thoughts, "but I'm content if we
never get back."

"It's not like we ever leave the past behind,
anyway," I say. "All our experiences, good and
bad, and all the people along the way—they are all
a part of us. We are who we are because of Mama,

Daddy, Dave, and all the rest. But the past is not where I want to live, either."

A comfortable silence stretches out as we drive along I-44 toward Oklahoma, each of us lost in our own thoughts.

Later, we cross the state line. "I wish it wasn't so long before we go to Galveston," Chris says.

We have a trip planned for October. We've rented a house right on the beach. For two decades, Chris and I have taken an annual sister trip, and experience again some of the natural delights we grew up with.

"The way time flies these days," I say, "it'll be here before we know it."

"It will be so nice to sit on our porch and watch the seagulls as the waves roll in. And those cute little sandpipers that skitter along, pecking at the sand."

"If you pull yourself out of bed in time, you can watch the sunrise with me. I hope we have at least one good storm while we're there. I can imagine sitting on the deck as a thunderstorm rolls in over the gulf."

She raises her brows. "October is hurricane season, you know."

"Ooh... now that would be exciting!"

Made in the USA
Coppell, TX
02 February 2020

15316204R00146